INDIAN CONSTITUTION AND EDUCATION

INDIAN CONSTITUTION AND EDUCATION

N.K. Chowdhry

SHIPRA

Rs. 850, US$ 42.50

ISBN: 978-81-7541-468-6

First Published in India in 2009

Indian Constitution and Education

Published by:

SHIPRA PUBLICATIONS
LG 18-19, Pankaj Central Market,
I.P. Ext., Patparganj, Delhi-110092, India
Ph.: +91 11 22235152/6152
Email: info@shiprapublication.com
Website: www.shiprapublication.com

If ever things go wrong under the new Constitution
the reason will not be that we had a bad Constitution.
What we will have to say is that Man was vile

—B.R. Ambedkar

Contents

Preface

The Constitution of India is much more than a set of Articles and Schedules. It embodies the ideals and aspirations of the people of an Independent Democratic Republic.

In order that young boys and girls grow up as enlightened citizens of the Indian democracy, they need to be imbibed with the ideals that have been set forth in the Constitution of the Indian Republic. The book contains comprehensive information on Constitution Provisions on Education, education of Schedule Tribes/Schedule Castes and other Backward Classes, Environment, Human Rights, Minorities etc.

The author acknowledges with thanks all the authors and their publishers which have been referred and quoted to enhance the value of the book for its readers and students of education.

1

Constitution of India: Select Features

1.1 THE BASIC PRINCIPLES

The Constituent Assembly declares its firm and solemn resolve to draw up a Constitution through which the ancient land attains its rightful and honoured place in the world and make its full and willing contribution to the promotion of world peace and welfare of mankind—Objectives Resolution adopted by the Constituent assembly on January 22, 1947.

Lord Mountbatten, Governor General of India, plan, comprised partition of India into India and Pakistan, was accepted by the Indian national Congress and the Muslim League. The British government accordingly passed the Indian Independence Act 1947 preponing the transfer of power from June 1948 to August 1947.

In 1946, much before the transfer of power, a Constituent Assembly had been set up on the basis of agreement between the cabinet Mission and the major political parties in India. The members of the Constituent Assembly were elected by the elected Legislative Assemblies. Out of a total of 385 members, Indian National Congress had 208 while the Muslim League had 73 members. With the passage of the Indian Independence Act, the Constituent Assembly gained a sovereign character.

The Constituent Assembly was not elected under universal franchise. All the same, the members were drawn from all walks of life cutting across party lines. The drafting Committee was headed by Dr. B.R. Ambedkar and assisted by prominent persons like Alladi Krishnaswami Aiyar, N. Gopalaswami Ayyangar, K.M. Munshi and T.T. Krishnamachari.

Starting from December 9, 1946 the Assembly took two years, eleven months and seventeen days to finalize the Constitution. The Draft Constitution had 315 Articles and 13 Schedules which in the final form had 395 Articles and 8 Schedules. Amendments to the draft constitution to the tune of 2,473 were debated and disposed of.

On November 26, 1949, the Constitution in its final form was adopted and finally inaugurated on January 26 1950 marking the 20th anniversary of the day on which at its Lahore session the Indian national Congress had set Swaraj as its ultimate goal.

A number of Constitutional reforms had taken place even under British rule during the 20th century. The one point that needs to be stressed while dealing with the Basic Principles of Indian Constitution is that constitutional developments initiated by the British Parliament were not intended to make India a free country. They were introduced more in the nature of administrative conveniences when Indian Independence India became free country, it was then that a Constitution was framed that mirrored the aspirations of the Indian people.

Like every other Constitution, the Constitution of India too aims at building up a structure of governance that is based on certain basic principles.

The foundation of the political system in India has been laid on the following basic principles:

Sovereignty Vests in the People of India

The Preamble of the Constitution begins thus, "We the people of India ...." The principle has been further strengthened by the provision of universal adult suffrage. The people are to choose representatives to the State Legislatures and the Lok Sabha at regular intervals.

The laws applicable to the people of India are those that have been passed by the elected representatives of the people. In matters of State, it is the will of the people that prevails and not the will of an individual or a group of self interested people.

Large sections of Indian people continue to be illiterate and ignorant. However the results of the past elections have established that the people of India have been exercising their right to vote with a fair degree of independence.

The Constitution gives every adult (21 years of age) the right to vote irrespective of all other considerations like education, property, sex, religious belief etc.

It also provides for an independent machinery headed by the Chief Election Commissioner responsible for holding free and fair elections. The Chief Election Commissioner is not subordinate to the Executive.

The secrecy of ballot further ensures that self seeking politicians do not have their way in rigging elections.

Socialist Ideas Influence Policy Decisions

The founding fathers very well realized that political freedom would be meaningful only if it also assures economic freedom. It was only in the year 1976 that the word Socialism was formally added to the Preamble of the Constitution. However the socialist objective is definitely set out in the Directive Principles of State Policy.

The Right* to Property is not absolute. The State can acquire private property in public interest against compensation. However the compensation paid by the State is not justifiable.

India as a Secular State

The Indian State does not make any discrimination on the ground of religious beliefs of any citizen.

No State Religion

Secularism should however not be mixed up with the state being anti-religion. All that a Secular State means is that the Parliament is not competent to impose any particular religion upon the rest of the people. Every citizen of India, subject to general conditions, has the right to enter any office under the State.

Fundamental Rights

Democracy at its best limits the freedom of the government by the will of the people. At its worst it offers the temptation for the ruling majority to claim that all its actions are infallible. If the State exercises unlimited powers over the individual, the individual will perpetually remain in chains. Unlimited political power to a body of men can lead to tyranny and negate all the good things that democracy promises.

Just as a car has one accelerator but two brakes, the democratic system too can be made safer by introducing two checks. The first check is that the individual citizen is guaranteed certain basic rights which can not be encroached upon by the State. The second is that the powers of the State is divided between two separate and independent agencies so that no body of men can exercise unlimited power

Fundamental Rights fall into the First category of checks on political power.

Indian Constitution grants to every citizen as many as seven Fundamental Rights. An important inclusion in these Rights is the provision that every citizen can approach the Supreme Court if he or feels aggrieved by any action of the State that infringes any one of his Fundamental Right.

Fundamental Rights are important as they set the conditions under which the majority can exercise its opinion.

Fundamental Rights grant to all Indian citizens a number of freedoms. These include the freedom of speech, movement and association, freedom of religious belief, equality before law, educational and cultural freedoms and the right to constitutional remedies.

---

* The Constitution of India does not seek to eradicate poverty by expropriation of private property. The State envisages multiplication of national wealth and resources and an equitable distribution thereof amongst all those who contribute towards its production.

The freedoms granted under the Fundamental Rights are however not absolute.

National security and general welfare over-ride individual's freedoms. Thus freedom of expression does not include freedom to preach against the very existence of the State. Every citizen is obliged to observe certain restrictions on his behaviour so that others too can enjoy their Fundamental Rights.

Directive Principles

The framers of the Constitution ensured safeguards of the life and liberty of the individual by providing for Fundamental Rights. They were equally concerned about private power assuming destructive directions. If too much of wealth was concentrated in the hands of a few individuals there is always the possibility of a revert back to the feudal system. With a view to provide for diffusion of economic power among various sections of the population, Directive Principles of State Policy were made an integral part of the Constitution.

These principles are in the nature of an agenda for future governments. The Central and State governments are directed to establish a social order and to inform all the institutions of national life.

The State does not have to answer for their breach in a Court of Law. But no party in power can afford ignore these Directives.

The State policies are to be directed for securing:

(i) that all citizens (irrespective of sex) have the right to earn adequate means of livelihood.

(ii) that the ownership of community's material resources is so distributed as to serve the common good.

(iii) that the economic system operates in a manner that does not lead to concentration of wealth and means of production hampering common good.

(iv) that irrespective of sex, workers are paid equal wages for similar work.

(v) that men, women and tender age children are not forced to work under conditions that would undermine their health.

(vi) That children and youth are in particular insulated against exploitation.

Directive Principles are in the nature of assurances to the people as to what they can expect from the Governments that assume power from time to time.

Independence of Judiciary

The framers of the Constitution were well aware that agents of the government could not be trusted to be just and impartial in situations where the government itself was one of the party to a dispute. They, therefore, created a judicial system that was independent of the Executive. Judicial independence is thus a basic principle of the Indian Constitution.

The independence of the judicial system has been ensured by a series of Constitutional provisions in respect of Judges. The Constitution lays down the qualifications, mode of appointments, conditions of service, and the procedure for their removal from office. Judiciary in India has all along worked with impartiality.

Federalism in Indian Constitution

Even in the pre-independence era, the country was administered on a two tier basis There was the Central government and the governments at the level of the Provinces. This system referred to as Federalism is most suited to a country that is multi-racial, multi-lingual and multi-religious.

Federalism involves devolution and decentralization of authority between the Central government and the State governments. However the Constitution specifically provides that in case of a conflict between the jurisdiction of the Center and the States, the Center would prevail over the States.

The Cabinet System

Under this system, the Executive wing is totally subordinate to the Legislature. We have a Prime Minister at the Centre and Chief Ministers at State levels. The policy decisions are taken by the Prime Minister and the Chief Ministers aided and assisted by colleagues referred to as Ministers. The cabinet comprising the Prime Minister or the Chief Minister along with other Ministers is jointly responsible for all policy decisions. Individual Ministers head different departments of the government. Their actions are subject to the scrutiny of the Legislatures. The Cabinet system ensures that policy decisions are taken by the elected representatives and also that the functioning of the Executive remains under the scrutiny of the Legislatures.

The best part of the cabinet system is that any time the majority of the elected representatives—the MPs or the MLAs find that the Prime Minister or the Chief Minister and his Cabinet colleagues are going off track, they can be removed by a Vote of No Confidence.

The Indian Constitution makes the Prime Minister the head of the Council of Ministers. He is not just another Minister in the cabinet. The other Cabinet Ministers are appointed by the President on the recommendations of the Prime Minister. In matters of appointment and dismissal, the Cabinet Ministers have been placed under the Prime minister.

Special Features

The school students need to know the special features of the Constitution so that they are able to appreciate how it has been different from the system of governance as it prevailed when India was under colonial domination. Reference will have to be made to these special features as the students learn more about the institutions and the system of governance in free India

All Constitutions in their main provisions look similar. The only new things are the Indian Constitution has certain prominent features which distinguish it from other Constitutions.

1. The framers of the Indian Constitution borrowed the best from the existing Constitutions and made modifications so that those shortcomings were avoided that had come to light during their working. It is a beautiful collage in which patches that meet the specific needs of India have been very artistically woven.

2. Many of the original features have since been modified by over 100 Amendments. In most vital respects the Constitution has been virtually recast.

3. It is a very comprehensive and detailed document. The original had 395 Articles and 8 Schedules. Over the years many more Articles and Schedules are added (Several provisions have also been repealed)

4. Indian Constitution is Federal in character. It is more flexible than rigid. For amendment, only a few provisions need assent from the States by way of ratification. The rest can be amended by a special majority of the Union Parliament.

The Constitution gives powers to the Parliament to supplement the provisions of the Constitution. A variety of modes have been prescribed through which the original text of the Constitution can be changed or supplemented without the need for a Constitutional Amendment.

For example under Article 17 of the Constitution untouchability has been made an offence. The punishment however is to be determined in accordance with the law passed by the Parliament in this respect. The Protection of Civil Rights Act 1955 thus supplements the constitutional ban on practice of untouchability.

5. The Constitution maintains a balance between Sovereignty of the Parliament and the Independence of the Judiciary. The Judiciary has been vested with powers to declare an Act as unconstitutional if it is in contravention with the Fundamental Rights. The parliament, if it so feels, can put the Act beyond Judicial Review by shielding it under the 9th Schedule which is a part of the Constitution.

6. Each Fundamental Right is subject to Legislative control. All exceptional cases like those where the interests of national security, integrity or welfare are involved are excluded. No case for contravention of Fundamental Rights can be made in such cases. Articles 31-A to 31-C of the Constitution provide for such exclusion.

7. The Fundamental Rights are not limited in scope. Apart from political and legal equality, the Rights also secure social equality. The prohibition of untouchability provided for in the Constitution is one such illustration.

8. The Fundamental Rights have been by an amendment to the Constitution circumscribed by Fundamental Duties. However like the Directive Principles, the Fundamental Duties too are not justifiable.

9. The Constitution confers on every Indian citizen the right to vote without any other qualification. The free and fair exercise of vote is ensured through the authority of the Election Commission.

10. The reservation of seats is limited to Scheduled Castes and Tribes. The earlier communal representation has been totally done away with.

11. The Government of India Acts in operation before independence had given the people of India some experience of the Parliamentary system of government. The Constitution has retained the system which is modeled on British Parliamentary democracy.

12. Indian Constitution is Federal but can be shifted to a unitary system if such an emergency arises. Indian Federalism is based on the principle that while he Constitution respects the autonomy of States in areas assigned to them, national security and integrity is of paramount and over riding interest.

13. It has since been ruled by the Supreme Court* that there are certain basic features of the Constitution which are immune from the power of amendment.

1.2 PREAMBLE, UNION AND THE STATES, AND CITIZENSHIP

> *The Preamble by itself is not enforceable in a Court of Law. It states the objects which the Constitution seeks to establish and promote. It also aids the legal interpretation of the Constitution where the language is found to be ambiguous —Supreme Court of India*

THE PREAMBLE

It would be very helpful for both the teachers and the students if the Preamble to the Constitution is explained word by word. All the distinctive features of the Indian Constitution emerge from the Preamble itself. For example, it starts with "We, the People of India ——" If this is elaborated it would be clear to the students that under the Constitution, sovereignty lies not with any monarch but the people of India. All other distinctive features can be similarly explained to the students focusing on each word of the Preamble.

The Preamble embodies the basic objectives of the Constitution and every Constitution begins with one. In case of the Indian Constitution, the Preamble reads as follows:

"WE, THE PEOPLE OF INDIA,

having solemnly resolved to constitute India into a

* Reference is to the case Keshavanada v. State of Kerala 1973.

SOVEREIGN, SOCIALIST*, SECULAR* DEMOCRATIC REPUBLIC,
And to secure to all is citizens;
JUSTICE, social, economic and political;
liberty of thought, expression, belief, faith and worship;
EQUALITY of status and of opportunity and to promote among them all fraternity assuring the dignity of the individual and the unity and integrity of the nation;
IN OUR CONSTITUENT ASSEMBLY this twenty-sixth day of November 1949 do
HEREBY ADOPT, ENACT, AND GIVE TO OURSELVES THIS CONSTITUTION."

As one goes through the text of the Preamble, three things stand out.

Firstly that the ultimate authority vests with the *people.*

Secondly the Objectives of the Indian Republic are Justice—Liberty—Equality and Fraternity

Lastly the Preamble declares the date of its adoption.

Does the Constitution reflect the will of the people? The matter did come up during the debates. The Constituent Assembly was not elected on the basis of adult franchise. Even after being adopted, the Constitution was not referred to the people for approval through a referendum.

It is true that the Constitution was not referred to the people for approval through a referendum in 1950. The task of ascertaining the will of the people would have involved elaborate preparations (electoral rolls) and expenses. For these reasons the no exercise ascertaining the will of people was conducted.

The results of the Elections held in 1951 provided enough credibility and acceptance of the Constitution. No one has challenged the Constitution since it became operative.

It was in the year 1976 that the words *Socialist* and *Secular* were added to the Preamble. The concepts were implicit in the Constitution even before these words became part of the Preamble. The Directive Principles of State Policy had enough provisions to bring about a socialist order. As for Secularism, a number of Articles within the original Constitution guaranteed India being a secular State.

Sovereignty: With the passage of the Indian Independence Act 1947 by the British Parliament, India attained the status of a Dominion within the Commonwealth of Nations. As the new Constitution was enforced, India became a Sovereign Republic. As a member of the Commonwealth, India has a free association with Britain but with no legal obligations what so ever.

- *Democracy* as perceived in the Preamble is very inclusive. It is not just the right to vote. In its broadest sense it includes social acceptance of all groups of people without any discrimination what so ever.

---

* Added in 1976.

It also includes economic democracy—a system of government in which all citizens have equal opportunities for economic growth.

- India is a *Republic* as the Head of the State is elected and the position is not by heredity as in case of monarchies. The Head of the State in the Republic is elected for a specified term.
- The Preamble lays down four specific objectives on of the Republic of India.
- Justice implies that the individual conduct of all citizens shall be such that it is in harmony with common good. All activities shall be directed to wards attainment of general welfare.
- *Liberty* in the Preamble means creation of conditions under which no citizens shall be subjected to any arbitrary restraint. Every individual have the fullest opportunity for developing the inherent capacities. The country would progress only when each individual gets maximum opportunities for growth and development.
- *Equality* and liberty go side by side. No two individuals have similar capacities and therefore the attainments of two persons may or may not be always identical. Equality refers to equality of opportunities for maximum growth of an individual's potential.
- *Fraternity* is imperative for ensuring the unity and integrity of the country. India is a country of wide diversities. It is only by promoting a feeling of brotherhood among all groups of Indian people that the integrity of the country can be maintained. All citizens irrespective of their sex, caste, religion or racial origin must feel that they are Indians This feeling can be best fostered by encouraging the feeling of or mutual brotherhood.

Indian Union and the States

The Indian Federation was not the result of any agreement among the units. The component units have no freedom to secede from the Union.

The idea of dividing a country into smaller units for greater administrative efficiency can be best explained by the analogy of a classes being divided into sections in a big school. India is a country vast in size. It is not possible to look after the various problems facing the people from any one central point. The country is as such divided into smaller units. Under British rule there were Provinces. Now we have the States.

It may be emphasized that a State can be best administered of most conditions within the territory like the language spoken by the people are similar. That has been the justification for reorganization of States after independence.

From Provinces to States

Indian Union, as already clarified, is not a voluntary association of States as is the case with United States of America. None of the Indian State can secede out of the Union.

Under British rule, the Provinces did have some measure of autonomy. They were however an integral part of British India.

As for the princely States, technically they became sovereign on August 15 1947. But on a negotiated basis they became part of the Indian Union.

The Constitution of India authorizes the Parliament of India to reorganize States or create new ones (Article 2). The area of an existing State can be increased by addition of territory or decreased by transferring it to some other State. The nomenclatures of the States can also be changed by virtue of powers vested in the Parliament under Article 3 of the Constitution.

Reorganization or changes in territory can however be introduced only after prior reference by the President to the Legislatures of the concerned States. This Constitutional provision ensures that due regard is paid to the sentiments of the people involved.* *Reorganization, changes in boundaries or creation of new states including changes in nomenclature do not amount to an amendment of the Constitution.*

It is to be noted that if a part of the Indian territory has to be transferred to another country, the provisions of Article 3 do not apply. In such a case there has to be an amendment to the Constitution.

There were four different categories of constituent units. The provinces formed the Part A States. The Part B States comprised the former princely States that had been integrated through negotiations. These were headed by a Rajpramukh (and not a Governor as in case of the Provinces)

The territories directly administered by the Central Government formed the Part C States. Some of them had Legislative Assemblies but the powers of these Assemblies were subject to the control of the Parliament.

The islands of Andaman and Nicobar formed the part D States. These were:

Under the direct and full control of the Central Government.

No one was happy about this three tier State system. Public pressure started mounting for a change and the first one came with the creation of the State of Andhra on October 1, 1953.

---

* In the year 1958, the Government of India and Pakistan agreed to transfer a part of Indian territory known as Berubari (West Bengal) in exchange of Pakistani territory. The matter was referred to the Supreme Court by the President in 1960. The court held that such a transfer could not be effected under Article 3 of the Constitution. Article 368 of the Constitution had to be amended to give effect to the agreement.

Reorganization of States

A States Reorganization Commission, appointed in December 1953, submitted its report on September 30, 1955 recommending the creation of 16 States and 3 centrally administered areas on a linguistic basis. It was passed in 1956, the number of centrally administered areas was increased to 6 and the number of States was fixed at 14. The States had been reorganized in a manner that each State had one Principal language as the mother tongue of the people of the reorganized State.

The total number of States now stands at 28 and 7 Union territories.

Citizenship (Articles 5-11)

Citizens refers to that part of a country's population who enjoy full civil and political rights. These rights are not conferred on aliens irrespective of whether they are friends or enemies.

The partition of India had created certain peculiar problems. Between the years 1947 and 1949, millions of people had crossed over from Pakistan to seek refuge in India. Hindus and Sikhs who had been born and domiciled in Pakistan but had migrated to India were to be given Indian citizenship rights. On the other hand Muslims who were born and domiciled in India but had migrated to Pakistan were to be put off the list of Indian citizens. The provisions relating to Indian citizenship are covered under Articles 5to 11 of the Indian Constitution.

Article 5 provided that at the commencement of the Constitution, every person who had his domicile in India and (i) was born in India or (ii) either of whose parents were born in India or (iii) who had been ordinarily resident of India for not less than five years immediately preceding the commencement of the Constitution was to be considered as a citizen of India.

Articles 6 and 7 related to persons who were residents of India but had migrated to Pakistan and those who were residents in Pakistan but had migrated to India. Migrants to India were further divided into those who came before July 19, 1948 and those who came after this date. All those who had come before the cut off date were to become citizens of India automatically at the commencement of the Constitution. The other category of persons were to become Indian citizens if they got themselves registered in the form and manner prescribed by the Government of India

Persons who had migrated to Pakistan but returned to India with the intention of permanently residing in India were covered under Art. 7 of the Constitution. Such persons were allowed to come back and settle in India under the permit system.

Art. 8 related to persons of Indian origin who had been residing outside India at the commencement of the Constitution. They were required to get themselves registered as Indian citizens with the Diplomatic representative of India in the country where they were residing.

Art 9 related to persons who voluntarily acquired the citizenship of a foreign State. Such persons may not be a citizen of India.

The Citizenship Act 1955: Provided five modes of acquiring Indian citizenship.

(i) *By birth:* The Act provides that every person born in India on or after January 26, 1950 shall be a citizen of India by birth. This however does not apply to children born to diplomats posted in India and those of enemy aliens whose birth occurs in a place then under enemy occupation.

(ii) *By Descent*: If a child is born outside India on or after January 26, 1950 and if his father or mother is a Indian citizen at the time of his birth, the child gets Indian citizenship by descent.

(iii) *By Registration:* The following category of persons can acquire Indian citizenship by registration:

(a) Persons of Indian origin who are ordinarily resident in India and who have been so resident for at least six months immediately before making an application for registration.
(b) Persons of Indian origin who are ordinarily resident in any country or place outside undivided India.
(c) Women who have been married to citizens of India.
(d) minor children of Indian citizens.
(e) persons of full age and capacity who are citizens of Commonwealth countries or the Republic of Ireland.

(iv) *By naturalization:* Any person not covered under the above stated categories can acquire Indian citizenship by naturalization. For that purpose he has to in the first instance renounce the citizenship of the country to which he originally belonged. Prior to the date of application he must have been residing in India for a minimum period of one year, immediately prior to the date he makes an application for naturalization.

The Act provides that the applicant must satisfy the Government of India that he intends to reside in India. Every naturalized citizen is required to an oath of allegiance solemnly affirming that he will bear true faith and allegiance to the Constitution of India as by law established.

Indian Constitution does not distinguish between a naturalized citizen and a citizen by birth or descent. Both category of persons have identical rights as citizen of India.

(v) *By Incorporation of territory:*If any territory becomes part of India, the Government of India may by order specify the persons who shall be citizens of India by reason of their connection with that country.

A citizen of India may lose Indian citizen ship under the following conditions:

(i) By renunciation (ii) by termination (iii) by deprivation.

The act makes special provision for children of Indian citizens who may renounce their Indian citizenship. Such children would cease be India citizens but can become a Indian citizen by making a declaration after attaining full age to the effect that they intend to resume their Indian citizenship.

The Act provides reasonable safeguards in order to ensure that no citizen has been deprived of his India citizenship except after following due procedure prescribed under the law.

The citizenship in case of India extends to the entire territory of India. There is a dual citizenship for NRIs.

Domiciliary Rules

In this context it is to be noted that permanent residence within a State may confer certain advantages. These advantages may be in the nature of admissions to and fee concessions in State educational institutions, eligibility to public services and even awards of contracts.

Domicile restrictions do not amount to discrimination.[1] The Supreme Court has held that that discrimination is prohibited only on the basis of race, religion, caste, sex or place of birth. Residence is no where mentioned and as such a State can confer special benefits on its residents in matters other than those in respect of which rights are conferred by the Constitution upon all Indian citizens.

In the State of Jammu and Kashmir special rights and privileges are conferred on persons permanently resident in the State. Only permanent residents of Jammu and Kashmir can acquire immoveable property in the State.

Domiciliary rules are a barrier in the way of establishing a truly single citizenship. However such exceptions in a particular class or classes of employment may be helpful in as much as local people are expected to have greater familiarity with local conditions.

1.3 FUNDAMENTAL RIGHTS AND DIRECTIVE PRINCIPLES

Fundamental Rights have created a new equality and have helped to preserve individual liberty. The number of Rights cases brought before the High Courts and the Supreme Court attest to the vale of the Rights. The frequent use of prerogative writs testifies to their popular acceptance

Fundamental Rights

The case for fundamental rights is based on the principle that while certain disciplinary rules are necessary in every society, it is equally important that the authority does not use the rules in an indiscriminate manner. When people feel they are being unjustly punished, the tend to stand up in revolt. A democracy therefore makes provisions for the Rights of the authority and the Rights of the individual. While dealing with Fundamental Rights, the teacher might take up cases from within the country or even outside where violence took place because the authorities disregarded the rights of the individuals.

General Nature of Rights

Over the centuries human societies have been alternating between tyranny and chaos and even anarchy in certain cases. If the State represented by a dictator or a absolute monarch gets unlimited powers, it leads to tyranny. On the other hand if individuals have unrestrained freedom to act, there is perpetual chaos. Time and again efforts have been made to strike a balance between the claims of the State and that of the individual.

The conflict between the need for individual freedom and State control becomes more marked in a democratic society. Civil liberties are fundamental to democracy. At the same time the State has to be empowered in order that equality, both social and economic, may be achieved. One way out of the dilemma is to give the individual certain Fundamental Rights that cannot be violated by the Executive or the Legislative wings of the government.

Why Fundamental Rights?

As more and more countries of the world switch over to democratic governments, the fear of despotism is fast receding. But the Legislatures and the Executive within the democracy are equally tempted at times to encroach upon the rights of the individual. Fundamental Rights as part of the Constitution provide a safe guard against such encroachment. The position is further strengthened when these Rights are put under the guardianship of an independent judiciary. Most countries of the world now accept the position that certain individual rights need to be made a part of the written Constitution and are also made justifiable.

Role of Judiciary in Enforcement of Rights

The Fundamental Rights act as limitations put on the powers of the Legislatures and the Executive. The Indian Parliament is a creature of the Indian Constitution. As such the parliament can legislate only within the limits set under the Constitution. The areas within which the Union and the States can legislate have been specified in the Constitution. In case any law is passed which transgresses these limitations, it can be declared void by the High Courts or the Supreme Court. The Constitution specifically provides that the State shall not make any such law which takes away or abridges the Fundamental Rights.

Right to Property

The right not to be deprived of one's property save by authority of law is no longer a Fundamental Right. An individual who feels aggrieved because his property has been taken away by an order of the Executive can no longer move the Supreme Court.

The adequacy of the amount paid by way of compensation where a individual's property has been acquired cannot be challenged before the Courts. The only exception is where the compensation provided by the Legislature is deemed illusory or confiscatory.

The right to acquire private property is not limited to just public purposes. The State can acquire an individual's property and give it to some other individual. or a private Company.

Other Laws Outside the Arena of Fundamental Rights

The arena of Fundamental Rights has been considerable narrowed down by a number of exceptions. For example a Law for Agrarian Reforms cannot be challenged even if it is violative of any of the Fundamental Rights. Similarly a law for implementation of any of the Directive Principles lies outside the arena of Fundamental Rights.

The Parliament can put any legislation in the 9th Schedule and there after it would be altogether immune from constitutional invalidity even though it may contravene a Fundamental Right.

Rights Arising out of Other Limitation

In addition to Fundamental Rights, the Constitution also provides certain rights to the individual which are justiciable. For example the Constitution provides that no tax can be levied or collected except by authority of law. If a tax is levied by the Executive without Legislative sanction, the individual so affected can seek redress in a court of Law. However since this not a violation of a Fundamental Right, the individual cannot directly approach the Supreme Court. He has to seek redressal by an ordinary suit.

Fundamental Rights in the Constituent Assembly Debates

The idea of a chapter on Fundamental Rights was supported by all sections represented in the Constituent Assembly without any reservations. Sardar Patel presided over the Committee specially set up for drafting the chapter on Fundamental Rights.

The members of the Committee were primarily guided by the ideals of the American and French Revolutions.

The Rights fell into two broad categories—public and private. The public rights included the right to choose the rulers and hold them responsible for their conduct. Another consideration was that the citizens should have a share in making laws that were to Private rights included right to personal freedom, freedom to follow govern them religious beliefs of one's choice, right to free expression of thoughts and the right to equality. Initially the Rights included the Right to hold property.

It was the considered opinion of the Committee that these Rights were essential for total development of an individual's personality.

A variety of Constitutions from different parts of the world were examined and their experience was taken note of. The Bill of Rights of the American Constitution and French Declaration of Rights of men were the two principal documents that influenced the members of the special committee.

There were a number of special situations prevailing in India that had to be taken into account. Firstly there were a number of disabilities from which the Indian people suffered due to their being subjects of a foreign government. Secondly Indian society was cursed by the caste system. Thirdly there were a variety of religious and linguistic minorities within the country. Some of the Rights were specially designed to take care of these peculiar Indian circumstances.

While the Rights to life and liberty were regarded as Fundamental, the Committee did not grant the same status of Right to education or employment. They did have the will but also knew that the Indian State in its present position could not guarantee these Rights.

Fundamental Rights were made justifiable. If any individual citizen felt that any action on the part of the Legislature or the Executive violated his Fundamental Right, he could move the High Court or the Supreme court for seeking relief

Human Rights and Fundamental Rights in the Indian Constitution

The Constitution of India incorporates the major ideas of the Declaration of Human Rights through the provision of Fundamental Rights.

The declaration provides for freedom of movement and residence. This is ensured in our Constitution by Article 19 which gives every Indian citizen the right to move freely, settle and reside in any part of India.

Article 14 of our constitution provides, "The State shall not deny to any person equality before law". This provision reflects the spirit of the Article 2 of the UN Declaration of Human Rights.

Other provisions in our Constitution which are parallel to the Declaration of Human Rights include Right of Freedom of Worship and Propagation of Religion (Art. 25), Right of conservation of one's Language and Culture (Article 29) Right of Equal Pay for Equal Work for both men and women (Article 39) and Right to have free and compulsory Education up to the age of 14 (Article 21 A).

Many more ideas of the Declaration of Human Rights are incorporated in the Directive Principles of State Policy.

RIGHT TO EQUALITY (ARTICLES 14-18)

The State shall not deny to any person equality before the law or equal protection of the laws within the territory of India—Art. 14

The State shall not discriminate against any citizen on grounds only of religion, race, caste, sex, place of birth or any other of them—Art. 15

There shall be equality of opportunity for all citizens, in matters of employment under the State—Art. 16

Certain acts like refusing any person to public institution, preventing any person from worshiping in any place of public worship or subjecting any person to any disability with regard to access to any shop, public restaurant, hotel or public entertainment or with regard to the use of any reservoir, source of water, road, cremation ground or any other place where services are rendered to the public shall be an offence punishable in accordance with law—Art. 17

The State is debarred from conferring any titles—Art. 18

Article 14

Many a revolutions have been motivated by the urge for political freedom and social equality. It is accepted that equality in all walks of life is fundamental to democracy.

All men are not equal in talents. For that one reason equality among all men and women remains a distant goal. It would be many decades or may be even centuries before humanity reaches the goal where all groups of people have equal economic and political opportunities for growth and realization of their maximum potential.

Indian Constitution assure its citizens a limited measure of equality. While political and legal equality form part of Constitutional provisions, matters relating to economic and social equality fall within the arena of Directive Principles.

Modern States exercise vast powers over the individual. The Right to Equality is intended to ensure that the powers of the State are not used in any discriminatory manner.

An important limitation with regard to Art. 14 is that it prevents discriminatory practices by the State. The makers of the Constitution felt that extending the scope of this right to private individuals will interfere with the liberty of the individual.

Article 15

The Fundamental Right conferred by this Article on an individual is a guarantee that he shall not be subjected to any discrimination in matters of rights, privileges and immunities pertaining to him generally.

No citizen can be denied access to shops, public restaurants or the use of wells, tanks, bathing ghats or places of public resort maintained wholly or partly out of State funds on grounds only of religion, race, caste, sex, place of birth or any of them.

It has to be noted that while discrimination based on place of birth is not acceptable, it is to be differentiated from discrimination based on residence. Residence as a qualification for purposes of employment is permissible.

The State however is allowed to make exceptions by way of making provisions for the benefit of women and children. Similarly the State is allowed to make special provisions for educationally backward citizens. Scheduled Castes and Scheduled Tribes are also covered under exceptions.

Article 16—Equality of Opportunity in Public Employment

The provision of equality of opportunity in matters of public employment reinforces the concept of universality of Indian citizenship. The provisions are more in the nature of a list of what is prohibited. The State shall not practice any discrimination on grounds of religion, caste, race, sex, descent, place of birth or residence.

There are quiet a few exceptions provided for in the Article. The Parliament has the power to prescribe the requirement of residence qualification for particular jobs at the State level. Exception also exists by way of reservation for certain jobs for backward classes.

Certain linguistic minorities have been extremely unhappy about how *permanent residence* is defined by different States*. It is contended that domicile restrictions very often exclude minority groups from public services under the States.

The States face a peculiar problem while conforming to the provisions for equality of opportunity in public services. On the one hand they seek merit. On the other they seek representation in public services for those groups that have been the victims of a social system that kept them backward for centuries.

The Central government has been constantly interacting with the State governments with a view to put into practice the ideals embodied in Article 16. For example it has been suggested that there should be no column for *caste* in official records. The States are also advised that backwardness should be assessed on economic grounds and not on just caste considerations.

Rapid industrialization and fast economic growth along with greater facilities for education are expected to create new jobs that would absorb a significant number of people from backward sections of Indian society. Such a growth would greatly help in realization of the ideals set forth in Article 16 of the Indian Constitution.

---

* The government of Maharashtra in 1974 issued an order to the effect that for certain jobs under the government, preference was to be given to local persons and a local person was defined as one who has stayed in the State for 15 years.

Article 17—Abolition of Untouchability

Such was the unanimity and enthusiasm on adoption of this Article by the Constituent assembly that the hall echoed with cries of "Mahatma Gandhi ki Jai." The Article does not create any special privileges for any group of Indian citizens. All the same this one Fundamental Right goes a long way in delivering crores of Indians from the curse of subjugation that they have been facing for centuries. The incorporation of this Article in the Chapter on Fundamental Rights asserts the determination of the people of free India to eradicate the evil of untouchability.

It was a strange course of destiny that the task of framing the Constitution of free India was assigned to a person who had himself suffered numerous humiliations just because he belonged to a caste that was regarded as untouchable. He had learnt his lessons outside the regular class rooms and had been thrown out of hotels in the dead of night. The drafting Committee under his chairmanship dealt a death blow this social curse.

In 1955, the parliament enacted the Untouchability Offences Act. It has been laid down that whatever is open to a Hindu has to be equally open to a member of the Scheduled Caste also. Any such act that interferes with the exercise of such rights is punishable with imprisonment up to six months or a fine up to Rs. 500 or both.

Social prejudices continue not withstanding the passage of the Act. The fight against the practice of untouchability needs to be carried to the hearts and minds of the people.

Article 18—Abolition of Titles

The State of India under this Article is prohibited from conferring titles on any person. If a title is conferred on an Indian citizen by a foreign government, the Indian citizen needs prior permission of the President of India for accepting such a title.

The ban operates only to the State. Public institutions such as Universities can confer titles by honouring men of merit. Military or academic distinctions do not come under the ambit of this Article.

The Government of India introduced four categories of decorations—'Bharat Ratna', 'Padma Vibhushan', 'Padma Bhushan' and 'Padma Shri', in 1954. These decorations are not to be used as appendage to the names. It is debatable whether these decorations have created another form of nobility.

RIGHT TO FREEDOM (ARTICLE 19)

> The most important among the inalienable rights of man are Life, Liberty and the Pursuit of Happiness
>
> —*Declaration of American Independence*

Liberty of thought, expression, belief, faith and worship are the desired objectives of the Constitution of India

—*Preamble of the Indian Constitution*

Why should the Right to Freedom be an important Fundamental Right? This can be very easily explained by the illustration that no one would like to be put in jail even if one was allowed all the comforts of life that are available outside the prison walls. Article 19 of the Indian Constitution guarantees to all Indian citizens a number of basic freedoms.

No one can be really happy if he is not allowed these freedoms.

The basic freedoms that make democracy meaningful are:

(i) Freedom of speech and expression
(ii) Freedom to assemble peacefully without arms
(iii) Freedom to form associations or unions
(iv) Freedom to move freely throughout the territory of India
(v) Freedom to reside and settle in any part of the territory of India, and
(vi) Freedom to practice any profession or to carry on any occupation, trade or business.

The need for freedom is as important as restrictions on their use. The restrictions must be reasonable. *Freedom of speech* cannot be equated with freedom to abuse. If every one is allowed to preach against the security and integrity of the country, the very existence of the State would be threatened. This cannot be allowed by any government how so ever liberal it might claim to be.

Apart from freedom of speech, the Constitution also ensures freedom of the Press. Although the word Press is not specifically mentioned, freedom of expression includes expression though any of the modern media like radio, television, newspapers and magazines etc.

The Constitution allows *Freedom of Association.* Workers can form trade unions. However people cannot be allowed to associate for carrying out activities against public order, morality or for conspiring against the State.

The freedoms guaranteed by the Constitution can be enjoyed only if the citizens also have the *Right to Free Movement and to Reside* within the country.

Citizens of India can move freely within the territory of India, reside and settle down in any part of the country. Reasonable restrictions however exist in the exercise of this freedom. The State can make laws restricting the rights of ordinary citizens to go and settle in particular areas inhabited by the Tribal people.

Considering that Indian society continues to be dominated by caste and professions based on religion, the framers of the Indian Constitution made special provisions that guarantee the *Freedom to practice any profession or to carry out any occupation, trade or business.* The State's power to restrict is limited to prescribing professional qualifications (like B.Ed.) for practicing any profession (like teaching).

Article 20 of the Constitution provides protection to all citizens against arbitrary or excessive punishment. *Conviction for Offences* has been put under certain restrictions.

Only a violation of law existing at the time of the alleged offence can be a ground for conviction. The penalty for the offence has to be limited to that prescribed under law for the specific offence. No person can be punished for same offence twice and no person can be compelled to give evidence against himself. These provisions protect the citizens against retrospective application of a punitive law and also against double punishment for a single crime or violation.

Article 21 provides that no person shall be deprived of his life or personal liberty except according to procedure established by law. The *Right to Protection of Life and Personal Liberty.* The Right serves as a check on exercise of executive powers in a high handed manner. It is to be noted that the Right to Life and Personal Liberty is not absolute. The Article does provide that these Rights are circumscribed by the provision that these can be taken away in accordance with the procedure established by law. A person convicted by a court of law to be hanged till dead cannot claim the Right to Protection of Life.

There are enough provisions in the Constitution to ensure *Protection against Arrest and Detention (Article 22)*. The person detained has to be informed about the reason for his arrest. He also has the right to consult and be defended by a lawyer of his choice. A person so detained has to be produced before a Magistrate within 24 hours of the arrest and can be detained further in custody only if so authorized by the Court.

Here too there are exceptions. A person can be detained if he is at the time being an enemy alien. A person can also be detained if a Preventive Detention law exists on the statue book

The second exception is considered necessary as India is still an emerging democracy and there are elements who have no regard for democratic liberties (like the terrorists).

RIGHT AGAINST EXPLOITATION AND RELIGIOUS FREEDOM (ARTICLE 23-24)

When the Constitution was adopted, exploitation did exist in many forms. There was the system of *beggar.* Landless labourers were required to work for free on farms owned by big land lords. In certain parts of southern India, Devdasis lived as life long victims of immorality. Articles 23 prohibits *begar* or forced labour. It has to be understood that a number of freedoms guaranteed under the Contrition would become meaningless if a person's life and liberty were to be at the mercy of another man.

The one exception to compulsory labour is when the compulsory service is imposed by the State for public purposes. Thus students being required to do Social Service as part of nation building programmes would not be covered under the provisions of article 23 of the Constitution.

No child below the age of 14 can be employed to work in any factory or mine or engaged hazardous employment. (Article 24)

This article is directly related to the provision contained in the Directive Principles. The State is called upon to enforce universal primary education up to the age of 14. This is possible only if provisions exist that forbid children in this age group being diverted to employment.

The preventive measures have succeeded only in a very limited way. Children continue to be employed as that is the one way they can supplement income of families that continue to live below poverty line. The same is true about sexual exploitation of girls. Immoral traffic continues for reasons that can be traced to extreme poverty among some groups and communities.

Religious minorities have been provided very generous freedoms under Article 25—28 of the Indian Constitution. The Indian Parliament is not competent to impose any particular religion upon the Indian people.

The following may be summed up as the distinguishing feature of Indian Secularism.

- The State does not identify itself with any one particular religion.(A fundamentalist State like Pakistan is an Islamic State where only a Muslim can be the Head of the State.) In case of India no such preferential treatment can be accorded to any one particular religion. The State does not practice any discrimination based on a citizen's religious belief and all public offices are open to all citizens who qualify irrespective of their religious beliefs.
- The *Right to freely practice and propagate religion* is subject to just three restrictions They relate to public order, morality and health.
- The Right to propagate does not include any right to forcible conversion. These are likely to disturb public order.*

In the *arena of Education*, Article 26 is a landmark provision. Every religious denomination has been given the right to establish and maintain institutions for religious and charitable purposes. They can manage their own affairs in matters of religion and have the right to acquire moveable as well as immoveable property and administer such property in accordance with law. The funds appropriated towards the promotion or maintenance of any specific religion are exempted from payment of taxes.

While according equality to all religions, the State is not bound to protect each and every religious practice.

Schools maintained or aided by the State cannot have compulsory religious instruction.

* Supreme Court in case M.H. Quareshi vs. State of Bihar 1958.

Educational institutional set up by trusts which require that religious instruction be imparted in the institution, are exempted from this provision. Denominational institutions have the freedom to maintain their religious character even when they get aid from the State. All the same even in such schools, no person attending such a school can be compelled to take part in any religious education without the consent of the parent

Within the country, there are a number of schools run by Christian Missionaries, DAV societies, Gurudwara Prabandhak Committees and many other religious bodies. While some of them are recognized schools, many others also get financial aid apart from State recognition. Thus the Islamic madarsas would be as much entitled to State aid as a Missionary schools or a school run by the DAV society however subject to such conditions as may be prescribed for recognition and grant in aid.

Institutions run by linguistic minorities do have students who do not have the same mother tongue. Usually the linguistic minority schools have their specific language as the medium of instruction at the primary level. They switch over to English medium at the Secondary level.

The educational institutions run by minority communities have been given some exclusive freedoms to accommodate the interests of minorities. However religious instruction in schools can only be given to those who are willing.

CULTURAL AND EDUCATIONAL RIGHTS (ARTICLES 29 TO 33)

The State shall not impose upon a minority any culture other than the community's own culture.

Article 29 guarantees the right of any section of the citizen residing in any part of the country having distinct language, script or culture of its own to conserve the same.

Section (2) guarantees that in matters of admission to State or State aided educational institutions no discrimination shall be practiced based only on religion, race, caste, language or any of them.

Section (1) of Article 30 states, "*All minorities whether based on religion or language shall have the right to establish and administer educational institutions of their choice.*" Institutions established or managed by linguistic or religious minorities are not to be discriminated against in matters relating to grant in aid to educational institutions.

The above Articles are in the nature of assurances to all minorities that the State shall protect the rights of the minorities to protect those interests that the minorities feel give them an identity and which they consider as fundamental to their living styles.

It has to be noted that the guarantees operate not only in respect of religious minorities but also cover linguistic minorities. Thus there may be grant aided schools run by a religious body like the Gurudwara Prabandhak Committee or a school run by the Tamil Education Society.

Every citizen of India has the freedom to select any educational institution receiving aid from the government. The parent has thus been given the right to control the education that his child would receive.

The parents, right are however circumscribed by certain reasonable restrictions. If a certain student does not have the required academic qualification he can be denied admission and that would not be unconstitutional since the refusal is not based on religion, race, caste language or any of them. A breach of Fundamental Right would arise only if the child does have the requisite academic qualification but has been denied admission only because he belongs to a certain religion.

The State retains for itself the right to impose reasonable restrictions of a regulatory character.

Minority right to establish educational institutions does not mean that they can establish institutions only for imparting religious education. Similarly linguistic minorities are not supposed to establish educational institutions for teaching only their language. Minority institutions have as much right to impart general as well as secular education as any other institution.

The Supreme Court* has further clarified that the argument that no conditions could be imposed on minority run institutions was unacceptable since right to administer does not include the right to maladminister. The State, as such, is entitled to insist that even minority institutions abide by such regulations as have been laid down for sanction of grant in aid.

There are another category of minority managed schools that are recognized but do not seek any financial aid from the State. In their case the recognition cannot be denied only on the basis of religion, race, caste, language or any one of them.

A number of other issues relating to Articles 29 and 30 have since been settled by the Supreme Court in various judgments.

The right of the minorities to establish and manage schools exists whether these schools are recognized and grant aided or just recognized without accepting any financial assistance from the State.

Whether a certain group or community comprises a minority is to be decided on the basis of the entire population of the area to which the particular legislation applies.

Schools run by linguistic minorities can impart education in the language of the children admitted to such schools. Thus Tamil could be the medium of instruction in a school run by the Tamil Education Society. Such schools also have the choice to have Tamil as the medium of instruction in the primary sections and English as the medium of English in higher classes.

---

* Reference made by the President on the Constitutional validity of certain provisions of Kerala Education Bill 1957.

For purposes of being recognized as a minority run institution, it is essential that it has been established by the minority and not otherwise.

Institutions established before the enforcement of the Constitution are equally entitled to grant of minority school status.,

Minority schools have a special responsibility by way of availing the guarantees under Articles 29 and 30. They have to make sure that education in such schools does not perpetuate narrow barriers between different groups of Indian citizens. While on the one hand they should preserve their distinctiveness, they must also ensure that the students coming out from such institutions cherish the same ideals and national aspirations that children from other schools do.

The very fact that minority is a term used but not defined in the Constitution has led to it being misused. Thus the Jains claim a minority status so that they can be out of certain restrictions that apply to other schools. Such demands can come from other religious groups, too, and would create more complications for the State Departments of Education.

Articles 29 and 30 have given the minorities adequate protection to preserve their religious/linguistic identities. Since religious and linguistic minorities are spread over the entire length and breadth of the country these Rights ensure that the Constitution does not become an instrument to further the religious and linguistic interests of just the majority community.

> *Of all the rights included in the chapter on Fundamental Rights, the Right to Property has been the one which has been subjected to the largest number of Amendments.*

RIGHT TO PROPERTY (ARTICLES 31, 31-A, B, C AND D)

The Constitution under Article 31(1) guarantees that no person shall be deprived of his property save by authority of law. The Courts could intervene if any private property was seized by any Executive agency of the State (like the Police) without proper legal authority. Any law passed by the State that seeks to deprive a person of his property could be valid only if it was consistent with the Fundamental Rights.

The State could acquire personal property only under two specific conditions. It should be for a public purpose and it must provide for payment of an amount to the owner either by fixing the amount or by specifying the principle on which the payment was to be determined.

RIGHT TO CONSTITUTIONAL REMEDIES (ARTICLE 32 AND 32A)

> *Article 32 is the most important part of the Constitution since without it the Constitution would have been a nullity. A declaration of*

- *Fundamental Rights would have been meaningless unless there was an effective machinery for the enforcement of the Rights.*

The mere existence of Fundamental Rights in the Constitution would have been meaningless in the absence of express provisions as to how these Rights could be enforced. Indian Constitution gives the judiciary the power to enforce the Fundamental Rights.

The Fundamental Rights insulate Indian citizens against excesses by the Executive and also against the Legislatures. Acts passed by the Union Parliament or the State assemblies can be challenged if they abridge any of the Fundamental Rights. Article 13 provides that the Courts are empowered to declare such legislations which are violative of the Fundamental Rights as void.

The Courts have also been empowered by the Constitutional provisions to issue writs in order to grant relief to an individual whose Fundamental Right has been violated by an Executive authority. The Supreme Court and the High Courts have been empowered to issue such writs for the enforcement of Fundamental Rights as given in the Constitution.

Article 359 makes a specific provision that the Fundamental Rights cannot be suspended except when a proclamation of Emergency has been made which again has to be declared only in a manner laid down in the Constitution.

The Right to bring a case of infringement of Fundamental Right directly to the High Courts or the Supreme Court is in itself a Fundamental Right.

The Supreme court acts as the citizen's guardian ensuring that the Fundamental Rights granted under the Constitution are violated neither by the Legislatures nor by the Executive authority of the State.

The Supreme Court is well within its rights to refuse to entertain a suit filed before it on the grounds that other remedies are available to the applicant. But if an application has been filed for infringement of a Fundamental Right, the application cannot be rejected on the technical ground that there are other legal remedies open to the applicant.

Writs to which a reference has been made in earlier paragraphs are in the nature of extra ordinary remedies in cases where no remedy is available under ordinary law.

As already stated, both the High Courts and the Supreme Court have powers to hear cases involving infringement of Fundamental Rights. The only difference is that the High Courts can issue writs against any person, Government or any other authority only if such a person or authority is located within the territorial jurisdiction of the High Court.

The Supreme Court on the other hand can issue writ against any person or government within the territory of India.

Any law which prevents the Supreme Court from effectively exercising its powers under Article 32 shall be void.*

---

* Gopalan vs. State of Madras 1950.

The Constitution authorizes the Supreme Court and the High courts to issue the following kinds of writs.

Habeas Corpus is in the nature of an order to the person or authority who has detained the applicant to produce the applicant in the court so that the Court might examine the grounds of detention and if they are illegal order the release of the applicant. The Habeas Corpus is a very strong and effective remedy against illegal detention of a citizen by a person or any Executive authority.

No writ can however be issued if the person detained has been convicted by a court of law on a criminal charge.

A writ of habeas corpus is also not issued when a person is facing proceedings for contempt of court or by Parliament.

Mandamus means "we order". The writ is issued as an order by the Supreme Court to the High Court commanding a person or a body to do that which is his, or its duty to do. Obviously the Mandamus can be issued only when the applicant has a legal right to the performance of legal duty of a public nature.

There are three essential conditions for the issue of Mandamus by the Supreme Court. The applicant must show that he has a real and special interest in the matter under reference and there resides in him a legal right to the performance sought. The Mandamus can be issued if there is no other equally effective and beneficial remedy available to the applicant.

A candidate has gone through all the formalities of selection and he has been declared fit for appointment but the authority concerned refuses or fails to issue the appointment letter. The candidate in such a case has a right to seek the remedy through a writ of mandamus.

Writ of Prohibition is issued to prevent a subordinate court from exceeding its jurisdiction or acting contrary to rule of natural justice. The writ cannot be exercised to restrain the legislative powers. It lies only against a body exercising public functions of a judicial or quasi-judicial nature. A judge hearing a case in which he is personally interested can be restrained by a writ of Prohibition.

Certiorari is a writ which orders the removal of a suit from an inferior court to a superior court While prohibition is available at an earlier stage, *certiorari* is available at a later stage on similar grounds. The writ can also be issued if the decision of an inferior tribunal is vitiated by an error apparent on the face of the record. In all such cases the High court can issue a writ of *certiorari* to quash the decision of the inferior tribunal.

Quo warrantor is a proceeding whereby the court enquires into the legality of the claim which a party asserts to a public office, and to oust him from enjoying it if the claim is not well founded. The idea behind the writ is to see that an unlawful claimant does not usurp a public office.

Where an applicant challenges the validity of an appointment to a public office, the writ is maintainable whether any legal or fundamental right of the applicant is infringed or not. It is very powerful instrument for safeguarding against the usurpation of public offices.

In certain situations the application of Fundamental Rights can be modified by Parliament. Article 33 of the Constitution provides that the application of Fundamental Rights can be modified in respect of Armed Forces and the Police Force with a view to ensure maintenance of discipline and proper discharge of their duties.

When a Emergency is proclaimed, the Legislature is competent to make any law and the Executive shall be at liberty to take any action even though it restricts the right of freedom of speech and expression, assembly, association, movement, residence, profession or occupation. As soon as the Emergency expires, Article 19 will revive. But the citizen shall have no remedy for acts done against him during the period of Emergency.

Fundamental Duties

The 42nd Amendment Act of 1976 inserted ten Fundamental Duties in Article 51A of the Constitution. Under this Article, it shall be the duty of every citizen of India—

(i) to abide by the Constitution and respect the National Flag and the National Anthem.

(ii) to cherish and follow the noble ideals which inspired our national struggle for freedom

(iii) to protect the sovereignty, integrity and unity of India

(iv) to defend the country

(v) to promote the spirit of common brotherhood amongst all the people of India

(vi) to preserve the rich heritage of our composite culture

(vii) to protect and improve the natural environment

(viii) to develop the scientific temper and spirit of inquiry

(ix) to safeguard public property

(x) to strive towards excellence in all spheres of individual and collective activity.

There is no provision in the Constitution or the enforcement of any of these duties.

It is hoped that if in any instance a Court finds that a Law gives effect to any of these duties, it shall be deemed to be reasonable in relation to Article 14 or 19.

Any law which gives effect to these duties would go a long way in serving as a warning to any citizen who indulges in activities intended to destroy public property or indulges in acts like burning the constitution.

Fundamental Rights—A Reality Check

A close view of the Rights reveals that some very important rights like the Right to Work finds no place in the list of Fundamental Rights. Moreover provisions like preventive detention and suspension of the right to constitutional remedies takes away much of the substance of the Rights guaranteed under the Constitution.

The Rights are hedged with too many exceptions and it is extremely difficult for an ordinary citizen to make out whether or not his case is covered under the constitutional provisions or not.

Amidst these criticisms the silver lining is that the Supreme Court has been providing protection against infringement of Fundamental Rights and this has had a salutary effect both on the Executive and the Legislature. Some of the Rights have been substantially modified in scope through Constitutional Amendments. On the whole the Rights remain a bulwark of individual liberty. The heavy costs involved in engaging legal counsels acts as a barrier to an ordinary citizen availing constitutional guarantees. One can only hope that with the passage of time conventions would evolve that will make the approach to High Courts and the Supreme Court easy for the common people.

1.4 DIRECTIVE PRINCIPLES

The Indian Constitution does not adhere to any one particular 'ism' but seeks to effect a compromise between Individualism and Socialism by eliminating the shortcomings inherent in uncontrolled private enterprise through social control and welfare measures.

The concept of Directive Principles can be traced back to the Declaration of the Rights of Man (France) and Declaration of Independence (America). These Principles were for the first time made a part of the Constitution in Spain and from there the idea traveled to the Irish Republic. The Constituent Assembly of India was influenced by the Constitution of Irish Republic and incorporated these as a striking feature of the Indian Constitution.

The Directive Principles are in the nature of Instruments of Instruction given to the Legislature and the Executive. These Principles cannot be ignored by who so ever captures power.

The Directive Principles also reflect the thinking on The UN Charter of the Universal Human Rights. At the time the Indian Constituent assembly was busy with framing a Constitution for the Indian Republic, the United Nations was discussing the Charter of Human Rights.

The Directive Principles contain a number of principles that relate to peculiar Indian conditions. For example the provisions dealing with Village Panchayats, cottage industries, prohibition protection against cow-laughter, Scheduled castes and Tribes are typically Indian.

The government agencies including the village panchayats are expected to follow these Principles in the governance of the country. The Directive Principles state the fundamentals for the realization of which the State must strive. The Preamble of the Constitution states the ideals for which the people of India need to work. These are Justice, social, economic and political: Liberty, Equality and Fraternity. These ideals are to be achieved as successive governments follow the path set in the Directive Principles of State Policy.

The Directive Principles are a part of part IV of the Constitution. There are 16 Articles (36-51) that deal with the Directive Principles.

The most important among those are the following:

(i) The State shall strive to secure and protect a social order which stands for the welfare of the people. It shall strive to minimize economic disparities and eliminate social inequalities.

(ii) The State shall direct its policy towards securing adequate means of livelihood to all citizens. It shall make endeavours to ensure that there is no concentration of wealth to the common detriment. Men and Women shall get equal pay for equal work and State shall ensure measures to protect the health and strength of workers. Childhood and youth shall be protected against exploitation.

(iii) Village Panchayats shall be organized as units of self-government.

(iv) Measures shall be taken to secure the Right to Work and in cases such as unemployment and sickness public assistance shall be provided

(v) Just and Humane conditions of work, including maternity relief, shall be secured.

(vi) Cottage industries shall be promoted and the State shall strive to secure a living wage along with a decent standard of life including opportunities for social and cultural progress.

(vii) The State shall take steps to secure workers, participation in management of undertakings.

(viii) Steps shall be taken to secure a uniform civil code applicable to the entire country.

(ix) Free and compulsory education shall be provided to all children up to the age of 14 within ten years from the date of the commencement of the Constitution.

(x) The educational and economic interests of the weaker sections of the society shall be promoted with special care.

(xi) The State shall pursue a policy of prohibition in respect of intoxicating drugs and liquor to secure improvement of public health.

(xii) Agriculture and Animal husbandry shall be organized on scientific lines. The slaughter of cows, calves and other milch cattle shall be prohibited.

(xiii) The State shall strive to improve the environment and safe guard forests and wild life.

(xiv) All monuments of historical importance shall be preserved.

(xv) The Judiciary in the country shall be separated from the Executive wing of the government.

(xvi) The State shall endeavour to secure promotion on international peace and maintain just and honourable relations with other nations of the world.

The purpose behind making the Directive Principles a part of the Constitution is to lay down the foundations on which an egalitarian Indian society could be built. The Principles seek to usher within the country a non-violent social revolution that would change the existing structure of Indian society to one which fulfills the basic needs of the common citizens of the country.

It is a matter of great satisfaction that the Supreme Court has held that even the Fundamental Rights could be amended to implement the provisions embodied in the Directive Principles. The only limitation is that these amendments should not offend the basic features of the Constitution.*

The Five Year Plans initiated soon after independence (starting 1951) are an effort to translate the Directive Principles into reality. These plans have, as their central objective, the promotion of rapid and balanced economic development.

However the country is yet to attain the status of a welfare State. All the same the country has been moving at a reasonable pace towards that goal.

The Directive Principles are not just platitudes. They are being systematically put into practice though not at a fast pace. The objectives that remain unrealized include full employment, State assistance to the old and the sick who are unable to fend for themselves. The vast multitude of people working in the unorganized sector are still without any cover by way of social security. Agriculture which contributes substantially to the nation's Gross Domestic Product and employment has been developing at much slower rate than the industries and the services sector. The slow growth of the agricultural sector is a matter of great concern as without that many an objectives set forth in the Directive Principles shall remain just a distant dream.

While making an assessment of the Directive Principles, we must keep in mind the enormity of problems and the limitations by way of resources and specially the work culture. Legislations alone cannot bring about social changes. Public opinion reflected through the results of periodic elections can go a long way in ensuring that only those reach the Legislatures who would be committed to further the objectives stated in the Directive Principles.

It speaks good for the health of Indian democracy that there have been no occasions when the Prime Minister of the country had ignored the objectives set in the Directive Principles. A situation in which the Governor or the President would not have consented to a Bill, because in his opinion it was against the spirit of the Directive Principles, has not arisen so far and is not likely to arise

---

* State of Kerala vs. Thomas 1976 and Lakshmi Kant vs. Union of India 1987.

considering the force of public opinion which no Prime Minister can afford to ignore in a democracy.

In case of a conflict between the Directive Principles and Fundamental Rights which should prevail? This question has come up before the Supreme Court more than once.

The Supreme Court is bound to uphold the Fundamental Rights because they are justiciable while the Directive Principles are not. However the one judgment that has been most relevant in this regard states, " If Parliament in its capacity as Amending Body decides to amend the Constitution in such a way as to take away or abridge a Fundamental Right to give priority value to the moral claims embodied in Part IV of the Constitution, the Court cannot adjudge the constitutional amendment as bad."

Every Fundamental Right, thus, becomes subservient the Directive Principles. Fundamental Rights guarantee the Rights of the Individual but these cannot be allowed to hamper the progress and welfare of the society as a whole.

India is to become a welfare State neither through a bloody revolution nor a capitalist oligarchy. The Directive Principles are revolutionary in character but the ideals set forth are to be realized in the constitutional manner.

1.5 PROCEDURE FOR THE AMENDMENT OF THE CONSTITUTION

During the debates in the Constituent assembly, Jawaharlal Nehru had observed that the Constitution should not be so rigid that it cannot be adapted to the changing needs of national development and strength.

The framers of the Constitution were inspired by the need for sovereignty of the Parliament, elected by the people of India, and as such prescribed an easy mode for changing those provisions of the Constitution which did not affect the federal system. Certain provisions of the Constitution can be altered by the Union Parliament in the ordinary process of legislation

Article 368 of the Constitution prescribes the procedure for the process of amendment in respect of other provisions of the Constitution.

In all cases of amendment of the Constitution, a Bill has to be passed by the Parliament by a special majority. Provisions which affect the federal nature of the Constitution have to be further ratified by at least half of the States, before the Bill is presented to the President for his assent.

An amendment Bill may be initiated in either House of the Parliament. When the Bill is passed in each House by a majority of the total membership of that House and by a majority of not less than two-thirds of the members of that House present and voting., it is presented to the President for his assent. As stated earlier, in the case of certain amendments, ratification by Legislatures of not less than half of the States by resolution to that affect is required before the amending Bill is presented to the President for his assent. The following provisions of the Constitution fall under the category where ratification is required.

(i) Election of President (Article 54), Manner of Election of President (Article 55) Extent of the Executive powers of the Union (Article 73), Extent of the Executive powers of the States (Article 162) or High Courts for Union Territories (Article 241);

(ii) Union Judiciary, High Courts in the States, Legislative relations between the Union and the States;

(iii) Any of the lists in the Seventh Schedule;

(iv) The representation of the States in the parliament and

(v) Provisions dealing with the amendment of the Constitution.

The procedure for passage of a Constitution Amendment Bill differs from the procedure relating to the passage of a Bill for ordinary Legislation. State Legislatures cannot initiate any Bill for the amendment of the Constitution. Constitution amendment Bills have to be passed by special majority and by both the Houses of the Parliament. The procedure for joint session, in case of deadlock, is not applicable in case of Constitution Amendment Bills. It is obligatory on the part of the President to give his assent to a Bill for amendment of the Constitution when it is presented to him after its passage by the Legislature. He cannot withhold assent as in the case of an ordinary Bill.

The word 'amend' in Article 368 has acquired a very special significance. It means only changes other than altering the very structure of the Constitution which would tantamount to making a new Constitution.

Thus no provision of the Constitution or any part thereof can be amended if it takes away or destroys any of the basic features of the Constitution. Judicial innovation has introduced a substantive limitation.

During the first sixteen years of the Constitution, it was amended twenty times There were compelling circumstances which led to constitutional amendments.

For example the 7th Amendment 1956 was concerned with the reorganization of States. The 10th Amendment 1961 integrated Dadra and Nagar Haveli with the Union of India. Goa Daman and Diu were made part of the Indian Union by the 12th Constitutional Amendment Act 1962. Nagaland was created as a separate State by the 13th Amendment (1962). Similarly the 14th Amendment made Pondicherry as an integral part of the Indian Union. Sindhi was recognized as one of the national languages of India by the 21st amendment (1969). Privy purses to rulers of princely States were abolished by the 26th Amendment (1971).

The two amendments that have generated maximum controversy merit a more detailed discussion.

The 42nd Amendment Act practically revised the original Constitution. The amendment provides that there shall be no limitation on the constituent power of the Parliament to amend the Constitution. The courts would have no say in the matter even if the amendment seeks to replace the entire constitution or its basic features.

However the Supreme Court has by its decision in the *Minerva Mills case nullified the attempt to preclude judicial review of the Constitution Amending Acts. The Court held that judicial review is a *basic feature* of the Constitution which can not be taken away even by amendment.

The other highlights of the 42nd Amendment Act were as follows:

(i) It introduced changes in the Preamble, and in as many as 53 Articles and also the 7th Schedule.

(ii) A Chapter on Fundamental Duties was introduced.

(iii) It was provided that if any law seeks to implement any of the Directive Principles, such law would be altogether immune from judicial review on ground of contravention of Fundamental Rights. This is exactly the reverse of what was provided in the 1949 Constitution.

The 43rd Amendment Act repealed those provisions which had been added by the 42nd Amendment Act to curb judicial review.

The 44th Amendment Act made the conditions of preventive detention more rigorous in the interest of individual liberty. Article 31 which deals with the right to property has been altogether omitted. The 42nd Amendment had made the duration of Lok Sabha and legislative assemblies of the State to six years. These have since been amended to the original position of five years.

There have been a number of Amendments since the Forty-fourth Amendment (1979).

The ninety-first Amendment 2003 restricted the total number of Ministers including the Prime Minister in the Council of Ministers to fifteen per cent of the total members of the House of the People.

In respect of States the amendment provided that the total number of Ministers including the Chief Minister in the Council of Ministers shall not exceed fifteen per cent of the total number of members of the Legislative assembly provided that the number of Ministers including the Chief Minister shall not be less than twelve.

It appears that the procedure for the amendment is too flexible. Any political party with a solid majority in the Parliament and in more than half of the State legislatures can easily amend the constitution to achieve political purposes or to get rid of judicial decisions which may not appear favourable to the party in power. Unless a very emergent situation arises, the process of constitutional amendment should not be resorted to for the purpose of over riding judicial decisions. Such liberties would create a feeling of irreverence for the Judiciary. The very foundations of a constitutional government would be shaken if the people lose faith in the effectiveness of the judicial system in the country.

---

* Minerva Mills vs. Union of India 1980.

1.6 GOVERNANCE AT CENTER

The President of India stands at the head of the Union Executive. He is indirectly elected under the system of responsible government introduced by the Constitution, real power vests in the Ministry. *It would have been anomalous to have a President directly elected by the people without giving him real powers.*

UNION EXECUTIVE—THE PRESIDENT

The Constitution of India is based largely on the British model. The executive powers vest in the cabinet supported by a majority in the Lower House which is directly elected by the people. The cabinet advises the President who is the head of the Union Executive. The President is placed above the party and symbolizes the impartial dignity of the Constitution. Apart from being the Head of the Executive, the President is also the Supreme Commander of the Armed Forces.

The Constitution prescribes the following conditions for a citizen to be eligible for election to the office of the President. He/She must

(i) be a citizen of India,
(ii) have completed the age of 35 years,
(iii) be qualified for election as a member of the Lok Sabha and
(iv) must not hold any office of profit under the Government of India or the Government of any State or under any local or other authority subject to the control of any of the said Governments.

The President's term of office is Five years. Within the term his tern can terminate by resignation or by the process of impeachment as prescribed in Article 56 of the Constitution.

In cases where the President is temporarily unable to discharge his functions owing to absence from India, illness or any other cause, the Vice-president discharges his functions until the date on which the President resumes his duties.

The Constitution provides the mode and ground for removing the President. He cannot be removed otherwise than by impeachment in accordance with the terms of Article 56 and 61. The charges for impeachment may be framed by either House of the Parliament. The resolution for impeachment has to be approved by two-thirds majority of the total membership of the House.

After such a resolution has been passed, the President has to be a given fourteen days notice signed by at least one fourth of the total number of members. The charges against the President have to be investigated by the other House. If the charges are established by the two-third majority of the total membership of the other House also, the President is impeached and removed from Office. the President has the right to appear personally or through a representative to represent his case in the investigating House.

Election of the President

The President of India is elected indirectly, unlike the President in USA. The electoral college that elects the President comprises of the elected members of the Parliament, and elected Members of the Legislative assemblies. The Constitution has prescribed a very detailed method for ensuring uniformity of representation of the different States and parity between the States as a whole and the Union. Each member of the electoral college does *not* have a single vote with equal value. Members in different State assemblies have different values attached to their votes. This was necessary as an MLA in every State does not represent equal number of voters. May be in one State 1 member may represent 50,000 voters while in some other State one member may be representing 75,000 voters.

The value of the vote of an MLA is determined by dividing the population of the concerned State by the total number of elected members in the Legislative assembly. The quotient thus arrived is divided by 1000. After doing so if the remainder is more than 500 then the vote of each member is increased by 1 and if it is less, the remainder is ignored.

The value of the vote of an MP is determined by dividing the total number of votes given to all the elected members of State assemblies by the total number of elected members of both the Houses of Parliament. The election is held according to the system of proportional representation by means of single transferable vote and by secret ballot.

The number of valid votes divided by 2 and adding 1 to the quotient determines a requisite quota.

Every eligible voter gets a ballot on which he/she gives first/second/third preference.

At the end of the polling the first preference votes for each candidate are counted in the first instance. If the first preference votes secured by a candidate exceed 50 per cent plus one of the votes polled, he is declared elected. If no one gets 50 per cent plus one first preference votes, the candidate who gets the least number of first preference votes is eliminated and second preference votes on his/her ballot are transferred to the remaining candidates. The process of elimination and transferring the third or fourth preference votes continues until one of the candidates secures the required number of votes (as determined by the quota)

Powers and Duties of the President

The President, as Head of the Executive, executes the laws enacted by the Legislature. His power extends to carrying on the business of the government excepting functions which are vested by the Constitution to any other authority

The Constitution requires that the ministers (other than the Prime Minister) shall be appointed by the President only on the advice of the Prime Minister.

It is obligatory for the President to act in accordance with the ministerial advice. The 44th Amendment has added a proviso to Article 74(1). The present position is that the President may require the Council of Ministers to reconsider such an advice but the President shall act in accordance with the advice rendered after such reconsideration.

Thus an advice received by the President from the Council of Ministers can be sent back for reconsideration If the Council of Ministers stick to their previous advice, the President has no option but to act in accordance with the previous advice. The power to return for reconsideration can be exercised on the same matter only once.

The powers of the President may be classified under the following heads.

- *Administrative Powers*: The President remains the formal Head of the administration. He does not have any power to control or supervise the various Departments of the Government of India. That is the responsibility of the respective Ministers. All the same all actions of the Union are expressed to be taken in the name of the President. All contracts and assurances of property made on behalf of the Government of India are expressed to be made by the President and executed in such a manner as the President may direct or authorize. The President has a right to be informed of the affairs of the Union even though he is not the real head of the administration.

  The Presidential powers include the power to *appoint and remove high signatories* of the State like The Prime Minister of India, Ministers of the Union, Attorney General of India, Comptroller and Auditor General, Judges of the Supreme Court, Judges of the High Courts in the States, State Governors, Finance Commission, Union Public Service Commission, Chief Election Commissioner and other members of the Election Commission and various Special Officers. Some of these appointments are made in consultation with persons other than the ministers. For example in appointing the Judges of the Supreme Court, the President also consults the Chief justice of the Supreme Court and other judges of the Supreme Court and High Courts as he may deem fit.
- The *Military powers of the President* include declaration of war or peace and the deployment of Defence Forces. However the exercise of such powers is regulated by the Parliament.
- *The Diplomatic powers* empower the President to negotiate treaties and agreements with other countries subject to ratification by Parliament. Here too the President acts on the advice of his Ministers. Indian representatives to other countries are appointed by the President. He also receives diplomatic representatives from other Countries and accepts their credentials.
- *The Legislative powers* of the President include the power to summon

or prorogue the Houses of Parliament and to dissolve the lower House In case of deadlock, the President has powers to summon a joint session of both the Houses.

After each General election, the President addresses both the Houses of Parliament. assembled together He also addresses the Houses at the commencement of the first session each year.

The President also has the right to address either House or a joint sitting and to require the attendance of members for this purpose. In matters relating to any pending bill or to any other matter, the President also has powers to send messages to either House of the Parliament.

- *Nomination of members* to the Houses is yet another function assigned to the President in the Constitution. Twelve members are to be nominated by the President from persons having special knowledge or practical experience of literature, science, art and social service etc. The President also has the power to nominate not more than two members of the Anglo-Indian community to the Lok Sabha if in his opinion the community is not adequately represented.
- *Previous sanction of the President to legislation* is required for introducing legislation on some matters. Some of these matters are a Bill for the formation of a new State or alteration of the existing boundaries of the States, a Money Bill and legislations

Affecting Taxation in Which the States are Interested

Assent to legislation is given by the President after a Bill passed by both Houses of the Parliament is sent to him for his assent. He may assent or withhold assent to the Bill,. Bills other than Money Bills can also be sent back for reconsideration by both Houses with or without a message suggesting amendments. In the last situation, if the Bill is again presented to the President with or without the suggested amendments, it would be obligatory on him to assent to the Bill.

Imagine a situation in which a Bill has been passed by both Houses and has been lying with the President for his assent. Meanwhile the Ministry resigns and is substituted by another Council of Ministers commanding majority in the Lok Sabha. If the new Ministry advises the President to use his veto power, it would be constitutional on the part of the President to use his veto even though the Bill has been passed by both Houses of the parliament.

The Constitution does not prescribe any time limit within which the President is to declare his assent or refusal. The President can exercise veto by simply keeping the bill on his desk for infinite period.

There have been situations where the Presidents have acted in a manner which refutes the allegation that the Indian president is just a rubber stamp.

In 1951-52 President Rajendra Prasad sent a message to the Parliament explaining his views on the proposed Hindu Code Bill. He explicitly said that he was personally opposed to the contents of the Bill but if adopted by the Parliament he would give his assent to it.

President Giani Zail Singh did not sign the Postal Bill 1986 although it had been passed by both Houses of the Parliament.

President Shanker Dayal Sharma declined to promulgate two Ordinances which were proposed by the government on the eve of General elections 1996.

Ordinance—making power authorizes the President to legislate by Ordinance in a situation where it is not possible to have a Parliamentary enactment on the subject immediately. This power is to be exercised on the advice of the Council of Ministers.

The ordinance has to be laid before the Parliament when it reassembles and shall automatically cease to have effect on the expiry of six months from the date of re-assembly unless disapproved by the Parliament earlier.

The Ordinance making power can be misused. The government is required to lay before the parliament the ordinance issued as an emergent measure within the time period prescribed in the Constitution or replace it with an act of the Parliament. Its duration can be fraudulently prolonged by issuing another new Ordinance on the lapse of the time specified in the Constitution. In such extreme cases a Court may invalidate the Ordinance.

The President has the *power to grant pardon* to persons who have been tried and convicted for some offence. Article 72 of the Constitution also gives powers to the President to grant pardons in all Court martial cases. The President may reprieve, remit, suspend or commute the sentence. The power to grant pardon also vests with the Governors of the States. However State Governors have no powers to grant pardon in cases of Court martial. Similarly the Governors have no power to pardon in cases of sentence to death. But the power to suspend, remit or commute a sentence to death, if conferred by law, remains unaffected.

Emergency Powers are the extra-ordinary powers that vest in the President to deal with emergencies. These powers will be dealt with separately as they deserve detailed treatment. The situations that would give rise to these extra ordinary powers are of three kinds:

Proclamation of Emergency may be made on the ground of threat to the security of India or any part thereof by war, external aggression or internal disturbance.

The president is empowered to make a Proclamation that the Government of a State cannot be carried on in accordance with the provisions of the Constitution. By means of such Proclamation, the President may assume to himself any of the governmental powers of the State.

The President is empowered to declare that a situation has arisen whereby the financial stability or credit of India or of any part there of is threatened. The object of such a Proclamation is to maintain the financial stability of India by controlling the expenditure of the States and by reducing the salaries of the public servants and by giving directions to the States to observe canons of financial propriety as may be necessary.

THE CABINET AND COUNCIL OF MINISTERS

The Constitution designates the President as the Head of the State. However for all practical purposes, the real executive authority is vested in the Prime Minister and his/her Council of Ministers.

The Prime Minister is appointed by the President. However he cannot act arbitrarily in the matter of appointment of the Prime Minister. By convention, the leader of the majority party or group in the Lok Sabha is appointed as the Prime Minister. There are situations when no single party or group commands an absolute majority. In such a situation, the President may invite some one who claims a majority in the House through a coalition. In such a case the person so invited to form the government is required to prove his/her majority in the Lok Sabha within a given period.

The Prime Minister recommends the names of the Council of Ministers, including the Cabinet Ministers, to the President for appointment. The President cannot disregard the choice of the Prime Minister. The Ministers hold office at the pleasure of the President.

The minister may be member of the either House of the Parliament. If a minister is not a member of either House at the time of appointment, he/she has to seek membership within six months or resign before the expiry of the period. The salary and allowances payable to the Ministers are fixed by the Parliament from time to time.

Composition of the Council of Ministers

The Council of Ministers comprises three categories of Ministers.

Ministers of the cabinet rank form a cohesive group who hold important portfolios. The cabinet forms the inner circle of the Council of Ministers. They meet frequently to formulate government policies and take important administrative decisions.

At the second tier are the Ministers of State. They have no say in policy formulation. The attend cabinet meetings only when invited. Their rank is lower than that of a cabinet minister.

At the third tier are the Deputy Ministers. They are usually attached to a cabinet minister. The Prime minister functions taking help from a number of specialized committees. In some cases the Prime Minister heads the Parliamentary Committee.

Powers and Functions of the Cabinet

Functions of the cabinet are spread over executive, legislative and financial fields.

The most important function of the cabinet is to formulate national policies in congruence with the declared objectives and programmes of the party. In the case of coalition governments, the cabinet decisions may be guided by the Common Minimum Programme agreed upon among the parties forming the coalition. The programmes need the approval of the Parliament but as long the party or the coalition commands majority in the Parliament, endorsement from the Parliament is no problem.

Apart from the national policies, the cabinet also takes decisions relating to the foreign policy of the government.

The Prime minister is the ex-officio Chair person of the cabinet. The cabinet takes decisions by unanimous consent. Differences if any are limited to debate during the cabinet meetings.

Every Minister of the cabinet heads one or more Departments of the government. Cabinet Ministers usually head important departments like Home, Foreign Affairs, Finance, Defence etc. Bills relating to particular departments are piloted in the Parliament by the concerned Ministers. The functioning of the various Ministries under the government is coordinated by the Prime Minister.

Bills can be introduced in the Parliament by the government and also private members. Before presentation in the parliament, the Bills undergo thorough discussion in the cabinet meetings. The ministers aided by their Secretaries reply to questions relating to their departments raised during the question hour.

Official Bills are given priority over private members' bills in Parliamentary schedules of work. The cabinet proposals presented before the Houses of the Parliament are seen through the various stages by the respective ministers. The parliament only discusses and approves the legislative proposals made in the Bill.

The cabinet is responsible for preparing the President's speech to be delivered on the first day of the first session of the Lok Sabha after the General election and on the first day of the first session every year.

All proposals for raising revenue by taxation and spending the same on government account are presented in the Parliament by the Finance minister on a yearly basis. The proposals are, in the first instance, discussed in cabinet meetings. Proposals for taxation and public expenditure are prepared by the respective departments of the government and then consolidated in the form of annual budget by the Finance minister.

When the parliament is not in session, the President issues Ordinances on the advice of the cabinet.

Similarly it is only on the advice of the Cabinet of Ministers that the President issues a Proclamation of Emergency. The Prime minister in his or her personal capacity may advise the President to issue an Ordinance or a Proclamation of Emergency but the President is not bound by such a personal advice. The President acts only on the advice of the Council of Ministers*. If the matter has not been discussed and approved by the Council of Ministers, the President is within his rights to ignore the Prime minister's advice.

Cabinet and the Parliament

There are several ways through which Parliament ensures ministerial responsibility.

Some of the more common devices are Questions, Budget discussions, discussions on reports by various departments of the government and adjournment motions etc. The most important device, of course, remains the Motion of No Confidence against the Council of Ministers. A Motion of No Confidence passed by the majority of the Lok Sabha members results in the overthrow of the Ministry.

Collective and Individual Responsibility

The Prime minister, as already stated, is the chairperson of the cabinet. All important decisions are taken by the Prime Minister in consultation with his/her cabinet colleagues. If a member of the cabinet or the Council of Ministers does not agree with the Prime Minister, he can be asked to resign or just dropped from the Council of Ministers.

The Council of Ministers is collectively responsible to the Lok Sabha. The Ministers are also individually responsible for the action of their respective department.

Working under the system of Collective responsibility, the entire Council of Ministers is obliged to resign if a Motion of No Confidence has been passed against it in the Lok Sabha.

If a mistake has been committed in a particular department, it is open to the concerned Minister to resign individually. However, whether a Minister shall resign individually or the whole Council would resign is a decision to be taken by the Prime Minister. As long as the Prime Minister commands a majority in the Lok Sabha, he is under no Constitutional obligation to resign.

The Ministers hold office at the pleasure of the President. It only means that none of the Ministers can claim permanence. The President being only the Constitutional Head, Ministers, in effect, hold office only as long as they enjoy the confidence of the Prime Minister.

The Prime minister is the first among equals. That may be so in theory but in actual practice it is the Prime Minister who takes all policy decisions. He/She may consult the colleagues but at the end of all discussions and suggestions it is the decision of the Prime Minister that finally prevails.

---

* Article 74 (1) provides *"There shall be a Council of Ministers with the Prime minister at the head to aid and advise the President who shall in the exercise of his functions acts in accordance with such advice."*

Powers of the Prime Minister

The powers enjoyed by the Prime Minister may be summarized thus:

(i) Choosing the team of Ministers and advising the President to appoint them.

(ii) Allocating portfolios and coordinating the functioning of the various Ministries.

(iii) Deciding the agenda of Cabinet meetings.

(iv) Acting as the link between the government and the President.

(v) Advising the President when an Ordinance is to be issued or a Proclamation of Emergency is to be made.

(vi) Making announcements on the floor of the House on policy matters.

(vii) Representing the country at International meetings and at International forums.

(viii) Acting as ex-officio Chair person of the Planning Commission.

The Prime minister is not an elected dictator. There are a number of checks to ensure that he/she does not over step the Constitutional limits in exercise of powers.

There have been occasions when the Prime Minister's conduct has been near autocratic. Such a situation can arise when he Prime Minister has absolute majority in both the Houses and a President who is very pliable. But for the period of Emergency during the ýears 1975-1977, Indian Prime Ministers have largely acted within the Constitutional limits, both in letter and spirit.

THE VICE PRESIDENT

If the Presidential office *becomes vacant, the Vice President will act as president only for a maximum period of six months. His main function is to preside over the Rajya Sabha.*

In the US Constitution it is provided that if the President dies in office, the Vice President takes over and continues till the full term of the President. However in India the Vice President can continue to officiate as President for a maximum term of six months.

The Vice President is elected by the members of both Houses of Parliament in a joint meeting. The voting is by secret ballot each eligible voter having a single transferable vote.

While discharging the functions of the President, the Vice President is entitled to same emoluments. allowances and privileges as the President.

The Vice President cannot be a member of either House of parliament or a member of any State Legislature.

The Vice President is the ex-officio Chairman of the Rajya Sabha. He performs functions similar to that of the Speaker of the Lok Sabha. In any situation where the Vice President is performing the functions of the President,

Deputy Chairman of the Rajya Sabha performs the functions normally assigned to him.

A number of Vice-Presidents have become Presidents but that is neither the rule nor the convention.

THE ATTORNEY GENERAL

He is the first Law officer of the Government of India.

The duties of the Attorney General include:

(i) Giving legal advice and performing other duties of a legal nature on such matters as may be referred or assigned to him by the President.

(ii) The attorney General also has the Right to speak in the Houses of the Parliament.

The Attorney General is appointed by the President. He must have the same qualifications as are required to be a Judge of the Supreme Court. He is paid a monthly retainer and receives such remuneration as may be determined by the President.

COMPTROLLER AND AUDITOR-GENERAL OF INDIA

He controls the entire financial system of the country both at the Union and the State levels.

He acts as the guardian of the public purse. He ensures that every Rupee out of the Consolidated Fund of India is spent as authorized by the appropriate Legislature.

The independence of the Comptroller and Auditor General has been ensured by a number of Constitutional provisions. He can be removed from office only on an address from both Houses of Parliament. His salary and conditions of service are laid down by the Parliament by law and cannot be changed to his disadvantage during his term of office.

He can be removed only by impeachment. He gets a salary equal to that of a Judge of the Supreme Court and is eligible for pension after retirement*.

It is ensured that he has no inducement to please Executive or the Union or the State during his term of office. He is disqualified from accepting any other office under the government after retirement.

---

* The independence of the Auditor and Comptroller General falls short of that of the Supreme Court. The Chief Justice of India is authorized to appoint staff of the Supreme Court but the Auditor and Comptroller General has no such powers. He does not have the powers of disciplinary control with respect to his staff which is appointed by the Government of India.

1.7 UNION LEGISLATURE—PARLIAMENT OF INDIA

The Constitution of India provides that the Executive power is wielded by a the members of the Legislature who command a majority in the popularly elected Chamber of the Legislature (Lok Sabha). The group, however, remains in power only as long as it continues to command a majority (Article 75). It is from this Parliamentary system that the functions of the Union parliament as the legislative organ of the Indian Union follow.

Functions of the Parliament

The foremost function of the Parliament is to provide the Council of Ministers responsible to the popular chamber (the Lok Sabha). Members of the Council of ministers, however, need not necessarily be members of the popular Chamber. In many cases the Council of Ministers comprise members of the Upper House (Rajya Sabha).

While both Houses participate in the formulation of executive and legislative policies, the power of bringing about a fall of the ministry, after it has ceased to comm and the majority, vests with the Lok Sabha.

The parliament provides the Forum for discussion and criticism of policies formulated by the Council of Ministers on the floor of the House. These discussions and criticisms not only enable the Council of Ministers to get advice from experts not belonging to the party in power but also enlighten the nation with respect to the errors and deficiencies of the government.

The people come to know about the functioning of the various departments of the government authoritatively from the debates and replies given by the concerned Ministers during Question Hour.

Article 207-208 authorize the parliament to make laws. Ever since the Constitution came into force, there have been numerous legislations intended to carry out economic and social development of the Indian masses.

The Parliament has the powers to levy taxes for raising revenue for public services. Through the annual budget, the Parliament raises revenue through taxation and other impositions. It also ensures that the money allocated to specific departments is spent only for the authorized purposes. Article 109 of the Constitution gives the dominant power in this respect to the Lok Sabha—the popularly elected Legislature.

Constitution of the Parliament

The parliament of India includes the President and the two Houses—The *Lok Sabha* and the *Rajya Sabha*; also referred to as the Upper House or the Council of States.

The President does not sit in either of the Houses but is a part of the Legislature. The only time he comes to the House is for delivering the opening address. However the bills passed by the Parliament get the force of an Act only after they have been assented by the President. While both Houses are not in session, the President exercises the power to issue Ordinances.

RAJYA SABHA

Article 80 of the Constitution provides that the Rajya Sabha shall comprise of not more than 238 elected and 12 nominated members. The elected members shall be the representatives of the States.

The 12 nominated members are chosen by the President from out of persons having special knowledge or practical experience in literature, science, art and social service.

The representatives of the States are elected by the elected members of the respective Legislative Assemblies under the system of proportional representation and a single transferable vote.

The Council of States reflect the federal character of the Indian Constitution. The number of representatives of the States to the Council of States varies according to the voter strength of the State.

The Council of States does not occupy a place in the Constitution as important as the Lok Sabha—the House of the People. All the same the Constitution makes no distinction between the two Houses in the matter of selection of Ministers.

In matters like making laws for providing for the creation of one or more All India Services the parliament is empowered to make laws if the Council of States has declared by a resolution supported, by not less than two-thirds of the members present and voting, that it is necessary or in the national interest to do so.

The Council of States assumes importance when it comes to passing Constitution Amendment Bills. Such a Bill has to be passed by both the Houses. The device of a joint sitting is not available in this case. The 43rd Constitution Amendment Bill had to stop at the Lok Sabha stage. The Janata Party had an overwhelming majority in the Lok Sabha. But there was no chance of the Bill being passed by a two-third majority in the Rajya Sabha where the Congress (I) and Congress (O) had an imposing majority.

THE HOUSE OF THE PEOPLE—LOK SABHA

The Constitution (Article 530) prescribes a maximum of not more than 530 members representing the States and not more than 20 representatives of the Union territories. Article 331 also provides that if the President is satisfied that the Anglo Indian community is not adequately represented, he may nominate not more than 2 members from out of the Anglo-Indian community.

(At present the Lok Sabha has 543 members from States and Union

Territories and a provision for two nominated members from the Anglo-Indian community.)

The underlying principle in determination of seats allocated to any particular State is that the ratio between the number and the population of the State is, as far as practicable, the same for all States.

The Constitution has adopted a system of single member constituencies for election to the House of the People. There is Reservation of seats at the general election for candidates belonging to the Scheduled castes and the Scheduled Tribes. (Articles 330 and 332).

Terms for the Houses of the Parliament

The normal life of the House of the People is five years but it may be dissolved earlier by the President. Dissolution may take place either by the expiry of the term of five years or by an exercise of President's power. The power of dissolution is exercised by the President on the advice of the Council of Ministers.

As for the Upper House, it is not subject to dissolution. One third of its members retire on the expiry of every second year. At the beginning of every third year, there is an election to the Upper House involving 1/3 of the membership of the Council of States.

Parliamentary Sessions

The Constitution (Article 85) imposes upon the President the duty to summon each House of the Parliament at such intervals that six months shall not intervene between the last sitting in one session and the date appointed for its first sitting in the next session.

Qualifications for the Membership of Parliament

Citizens of India who do not stand disqualified otherwise are eligible to be a candidate for election to the Lok Sabha provided they have attained the age of 25 years. The minimum age for entry to Rajya Sabha is 30 years.

A person holding any office of profit other than those exempted by the Parliament stands disqualified for membership of the Parliament. If a question arises whether or not a person stands disqualified, the President's decision in this regard is final. The President seeks the opinion of the Election Commission in this regard as provided for in Article 103 of the Constitution.

The Constitution does not allow dual membership. If a person gets elected to the Parliament he has to resign his seat in the State Legislature if he/she already holds one.

The salaries, allowances and pensions of the members of the parliament are governed by the Act of 1954 as amended from time to time.

Speaker

Article 93 of the Constitution provides that after the first sitting the Lok Sabha shall chose the Speaker and the Deputy Speaker. The Speaker presides over the proceedings of the House but does not have the Right to Vote except in the case of equality of vote.

The Speaker has the final power to maintain order within the House and to interpret the Rules of Procedure. The Speaker's conduct is not subject to the jurisdiction of any court.

When a joint session of the both Houses of the Parliament takes place, the Speaker of the House of the People presides over the proceedings.

When a Money Bill is sent to the Upper House after having been passed by the Lok Sabha, the Speaker certifies that it is money Bill.

In the absence of the Speaker, the Deputy Speaker conducts the proceedings of the House.

Chairman—Council of States

The Vice President is the ex-officio Chairman of the Upper House and performs functions similar to those of the Speaker. But he is not elected by the members of the Rajya Sabha. When he officiates as the President of India, his functions are performed by the Deputy Chairman.

Privileges

Indian Parliament has so far not passed any legislation codifying the privileges and immunities of the Members of the Parliament. The privileges of the Members of the Indian Parliament are the same as those of the members of the House of Commons in Britain. It is also provided that in case there is a conflict between the privileges of the Parliament and Fundamental Rights, the former shall prevail. For example if the Speaker of the Lok Sabha decides to expunge certain parts of the speech delivered by a member on the floor of the House, the member cannot claim the protection of the Right to Freedom of expression.

Apart from freedom of speech, the members enjoy certain other privileges, too. They cannot be arrested during the continuance of a meeting of the Chamber or a Committee of which he is a member. However arrest for a criminal offence is not covered under this provision. The Speaker has to be immediately informed if a Member of the Lok Sabha is arrested on a criminal charge.

The member of the Parliament cannot be made liable in any court in respect of any thing said on the floor of the House. This freedom is, however, subject to the Rules of Procedure of the House.

The conduct of a judge of the High Court or the Supreme Court cannot be discussed or referred to in the parliament except during the course of a debate on impeachment of the judge.

Each House of the Parliament has the power to punish members and outsiders for breach of privileges. The punishment could be in the form a admonition, reprimand or imprisonment.

Legislative Procedure

In the first stage a Bill (other than money Bill) may be introduced in either of the two Houses. The Bill may be introduced by a minister or even a Private member.

In the next stage the member in charge may make any of the following motions:

(a) The Bill be taken into consideration,
(b) It be referred to a Select Committee,
(c) It be refereed to a Joint Committee of both Houses of the Parliament and,
(d) The Bill be circulated for eliciting public opinion.

If a Bill s refereed to a Select Committee, the next stage in the passage of the Bill is that the after the receipt of the report of the Select Committee the clauses of the Bill become open for consideration along with any amendments that may be moved.

In the final stage, the Bill is taken into consideration and after the amendments if any the Bill is carried and taken as passed.

The Bill is then transmitted to the other House. here again it undergoes all the stages as in the originating House. It may be rejected in which case a joint sitting may be called by the President. In case the Bill is passed with amendments it goes to the originating House. If the originating House does not accept the amendments, there is a case for joint session. In case the amendments are acceptable, it is presented to the President for his assent.

If the President gives his assent, the Bill becomes an Act. The next thing is for the government to notify it in the Government Gazette.

If the president does not assent, he may send the Bill back for reconsideration. However if the House passes the Bill again with or without the suggested amendments, the President has no power to withhold his assent.

Money Bills are those bills that deal with taxes, borrowing, income, expenditure, grants etc from the Consolidated Fund of India. With regard to Money Bills the powers of the two Houses are different.:

Money Bills can be introduced only in the Lok Sabha. After it is passed in Lok Sabha, it goes to the Rajya Sabha. The Rajya Sabha has to send it back within 14 days with its recommendations, if any. These recommendations may or may not be accepted by the Lok Sabha. The Rajya Sabha thus plays only an advisory role so far as Money Bills are concerned.

Procedure for joint sitting of both Houses: A joint sitting cannot be resorted to for passing a Constitution Amendment Bill*. Joint sittings may be convened in case of a deadlock between the two Houses of the Parliament. A bill passed by the majority of the total members of both Houses present and voting is deemed to have been passed by both the Houses.**

Financial Procedure

The *annual budget* is the most important among the Money Bills.

The budget is the annual financial statement of income and expenditure of the Union government. The Financial year extends from April 1 to March 31 (next year). Before the commencement of the financial year, each year the Minister for Finance, with the approval of the President, causes the budget to be presented before the Lok Sabha. The budget contains a review of the financial health of the government along with an estimate of receipts and proposed expenditure for the ensuing financial year. It also contains proposals for taxation and proposed means for meeting the expenditure for the coming year.

On the following days, after the presentation, the items included in the budget are discussed and debated. After the debates and discussions are over, estimates of proposed expenditure during the ensuing financial year are submitted in the Lok Sabha. The expenditure is made up of two distinct categories. Salaries and allowances of the President, Vice President, Speaker, Supreme Court Judges and all other items similarly mentioned in the Constitution are charged on the Consolidated Fund of India. These items are not subject to debate since the payments are guaranteed by the Constitution. All other items of expenditure are to be covered under demands for grants. The demands are presented by the respective Ministers who make explanatory speeches to justify their demand for grants. The Speaker after consulting the Leader of the House allots a number of days for voting of grants. The opposition may move amendments for a cut in the grant. But such cut motions have to be defeated by the party in power. In some cases the amendments are withdrawn after the opposition members have made their point in the Lok Sabha debate. On some occasions the Minister may agree to roll back a proposal. On the last date of the debate, the demands for grants are put to vote.

---

* The Constitution 64th Amendment Bill 1989 and the 65th Amendment Bill 1989 could not be passed as these could not secure the requisite majority in the Rajya Sabha even though they had been passed in the Lok Sabha.

** Dowry Prohibition Bill 1961 and banking Services Commission (repeal) Bill 1978 were passed in the joint sitting of both the Houses of the Parliament.

After all demands for grants have been put and debated in the House, an Appropriation Bill is introduced in the Lok Sabha. The Bill has to be passed by both the Houses of the Parliament. Thereafter the Bill goes to the Rajya Sabha. The Rajya Sabha has to send back the Bill within 14 days with or without suggesting amendments. The Rajya Sabha cannot hold the Bill and if the same is not returned back within the stipulated time, it is taken as having been passed by the Upper House.

The Appropriation Act fixes the amount which can be drawn out of the Consolidated Fund for meeting expenditure against each grant.

There is still one more formality connected with the provision of funds to the government. Apart from the Appropriation Act, there is the Finance Act. The Act deals with the legislation which authorizes the raising of funds through taxation as contained in the financial proposals put before the Parliament for the ensuing financial year.

The two committees—*Estimates Committee and the Public Accounts Committee* play an important role in the financial procedure.

The Committee of Estimates is responsible for scrutinizing the expenditure proposed by the Government., After the presentation of the annual Financial Statement, the Committee examines the estimates and reports to the House what economies, improvements in organization or administrative reforms may be effected consistent with the government policies.

The Public Accounts Committee examines the report of the Auditor and Comptroller General. The Committee is expected to satisfy itself that the money shown in the accounts as having been disbursed were legally available for and applicable to the service or purpose for which they have been charged. The Committee submits its report to the House of the people so that the irregularities if any noticed by it may be discussed by Parliament and effective steps taken to ensure that such irregularities are not repeated.

By an Act of 1950, Contingency Fund for India has been created and put at the disposal of the executive to enable advances to be made from time to time for the purpose of meeting unforeseen expenditure.

UNION JUDICIARY—THE SUPREME COURT

The Supreme Court under the Federal Constitution is the independent and impartial authority to settle all disputes between the Centre and the States about the terms of the division of power. It is the highest interpreter of the Constitution. The Supreme Court of India performs the most important function of being the final tribunal for determination of disputes as may arise between the Center and the States.

The Supreme Court of India is constituted under Article 124 of the Constitution and initially had one Chief Justice and seven other judges. The

Parliament has the authority to change the number of Judges from time to time. The Constitution also provides that Judges may be appointed on an adhoc basis whenever necessary. If necessary, the retired judges of the Supreme Court and the High Court can also be called upon to act as Judges of the Supreme Court.

Qualifications for Appointment as Judges

For appointment as a judge of the Supreme Court, the person should be:

(a) citizen of India, and

(b) either:

  (i) a distinguished jurist or

  (ii) has been a High Court Judge for at least 5 years or

  (iii) has been an advocate of a High Court for at least ten years.

Appointment and Term of Office

Judges of the Supreme Court are appointed by the President in consultation with the Chief Justice of the Supreme Court. The Judges hold office till the age of 65. They can resign their office by writing addressed to the President.

Salaries

The salaries payable to the Judges of the Supreme Court (and the Chief Justice) are not fixed by the Legislature but are a part of the Constitution. Each Judge is entitled to a rent free accommodation along with certain other allowances and privileges. The salary, allowances, privileges and the rights in respect of pension after retirement cannot be varied to the disadvantage of a Judge after his retirement.

The Supreme Court is also authorized to have its own establishment. All appointments of officers and servants of the Supreme Court are made by the Chief Justice or any other judge or officer so authorized by the Chief Justice.

Independence of the Judges

The independence of the Judges is sought to be secured by a number of specific provisions in the Constitution.

The appointments of judges of the Supreme Court have been insulated from the realm of pure politics by providing that President is to consult the Chief Justice of the Supreme Court in this respect.

A judge of the Supreme Court can be removed from office only upon an address to that effect being passed by a special majority of each House of the Parliament. The only grounds for impeachment are proven misbehaviour and incapacity.

The salaries etc. of the Judges are not subject to vote in the parliament.

The parliament is forbidden from discussing the conduct of a Judge of the

Supreme Court except upon a motion for address to the President for the removal of the Judge.

After retirement a judge of the Supreme Court is not permitted to plead or act in any Court or before any authority within the territory of India.*

Powers of the Supreme Court

The jurisdiction of the Supreme Court is three fold—*Original-Appellate and Advisory.*

Article 131 of the Constitution gives the Supreme Court of India exclusive jurisdiction in any dispute between the Union government and a State or between any two or more States of the Union. This *original jurisdiction* is, however, invoked only if the dispute involves a question of law or fact on which depends the existence of a legal right which the Court is called upon to determine.

An appeal to the Court lies from any judgment or decree or final order of the court, civil, criminal or any other proceeding subject to the provision that the High Court certifies that a substantial question of law or constitution is involved. The Supreme Court is the final authority in every matter that involves interpretation of the Constitution.

The appellate jurisdiction of the Supreme court in civil cases is determined by the value of the subject matter under dispute. Before the case is taken up by the Supreme Court, the High Court, that heard the case initially, has to certify that the value of the subject matter of the dispute is not less than an amount fixed by the relevant Article. The Parliament is empowered to enlarge the appellate jurisdiction of the Supreme Court in civil cases.

In all cases where a death sentence has been passed by a High court, in a case in which the accused had been initially acquitted, an appeal shall lie before the Supreme Court.

An appeal also lies before the Supreme Court in cases in which the concerned High Court certifies that it is fit case for appeal.

While considering matters related to interpretation of the Constitution, the Supreme Court bench usually comprises five or more judges. Three or even two judges hear civil and criminal appeals.

The Supreme Court under provisions contained in Article 136 Court may, in its discretion, grant *special leave to appeal* from any judgment, decree or sentence in any cause passed by any court or tribunal. Courts constituted under any law relating to Armed forces are an exception.

---

* There is, however, no bar against a retired judge being appointed to any other office under the Government. The expectation of such appointment indirectly detracts from the independence of the judiciary. In the past retired judges of the Supreme Court have been appointed to hold offices like Governor, Ambassador etc. under the government. In addition retired judges have ben, in the past, been appointed to a number of Boards and Commissions.

The reach of Article 136 has become a convenient instrument, at the disposal of the Supreme Court, to check acts of unjust decisions by administrative tribunals that are set up by the government from time to time.

Article 143 empowers the President to refer to the Supreme Court any question of law or a question of fact that is of public importance for opinion and consultation. The Supreme Court however is under no constitutional obligation to give its opinion or advice in the matter referred to by the President.*

The Constitution provides the Supreme Court powers to issue directions or writs for enforcement of Fundamental Rights. In addition to that Article 32 empowers the Parliament to confer on the Supreme Court supplementary powers to enable the court to exercise its jurisdiction effectively.

What if the Supreme Court goes wrong?

Article 137 empowers the Court to review its own judgments and orders.

1.8 GOVERNANCE AT STATES

THE STATE EXECUTIVE

The executive power is vested in the Council of Ministers. If the Governor were to be elected, as originally proposed in the Draft Constitution, he might have considered himself superior to the Chief Minister. He could have at his discretion come forward and intervened in the governance of the State leading to a surrender of democracy.

There is much congruence between governance at the level of States and at the Center.

The Chief Minister in the State is the counterpart of the Prime Minister in the Union government. State legislatures are modeled more or less on the same pattern as the Parliament. The apex judicial court at the State level, designated as the High Court, occupies the same status within the State as the Supreme Court for the Indian Union.

The Governor

This is not to say that governance at the State level is in all respects identical to that the Center. The Governor is the Head of the Executive at the State level and is appointed (and not elected like the President) by the President of India. The normal period for which a Governor occupies office is five years.

---

* In 1958, an agreement was reached between the Prime Ministers of India and Pakistan. The two countries were to exchange territories under the terms of the agreement. The matter was referred to the Supreme Court which declared that a Constitutional Amendment was necessary for transfer of Indian territory to foreign State.

Qualifications for Appointment: Citizens of India who have completed the age of 35 years are eligible for being appointed as Governor. The Governor is not a member of either House of the State Legislature nor can hold any office of profit under the State Government.

Salary etc. and Mode of Appointment: He is entitled to free residential accommodation and a salary and other allowances as may be fixed from time to time. The salary of the Governor is not voted in the Parliament being charged to the Consolidated Fund of India.

The Constitution vests the power of appointing Governors in the President. In effect it means that the Governor is an appointee of the Central government. Normally a person appointed as a Governor does not belong to the State to which he is appointed. The Central government does not even, by convention, consult State governments in matters relating to the appointment of Governor. Appointment of persons formerly involved in active party politics has often been a cause for conflict between the State governments and the Center.

A governor of the a State can be dismissed even for political reasons as the Prime Minister can advise the President to do so without assigning any reason or cause under Article 156(1).

Powers and Functions of the Governor: The Governor in many respects plays roles similar to those played by the President at the Union level. The Chief Minister and other members of the Council of Ministers are appointed by the Governor and hold office at his pleasure. In normal circumstances a Chief Minister continues to remain in office as long as he enjoys a majority support in the Vidhan Sabha or the lower House of the State.

All executive actions of the State are taken in the name of the Governor. Other officers of the State like the Advocate General are appointed by the Governor.

The Governor is vested with the power to grant pardon to persons who may have been convicted of any offence against any law in a matter to which the executive power of the State extends.

The Governor is an integral part of the State Legislature. State assembly sessions are convened by the Governor and he addresses the Legislatures in person or just sends his message. Bills passed by the Stet Legislatures go to the respective Governors for assent.

When a Bill duly passed by the Legislature is received by the Governor, he may assent to it, send it back for reconsideration or forward it to the President. Money Bills, however, cannot be returned for reconsideration by the Legislature.

If the Governor is satisfied that there exist circumstances which make it necessary for him to take immediate action, he has the power to issue an Ordinance when the Legislature is not in session.

The Ordinance issued by the Governor has the same force as an Act passed by the Legislature for the time it is enforced. Ordinances issued when the Legislature is not in session have to be laid before the House for approval and becomes invalid in case the House does not approve it. Ordinances cannot be issued in respect of provisions which are outside the powers of the Governor.

The Governor has powers to appoint Judges of the State High Court. Article 217 however provides that he is entitled to be consulted by the President in the matter.

The Governor can nominate one member of the Anglo-Indian community to the Legislature in case he is satisfied that the community is not adequately represented.

When a State is put under President's Rule, the Governor assumes full control over the State administration. The State, during the period of such an emergency, is run with the help of civil services.

Governor and the Council of Ministers: In exercise of the functions assigned to him by the Constitution, the Governor acts on the advice of the Council of Ministers. The advice that is rendered to the Governor cannot be the subject of any enquiry by any court of law.

While the Constitution does not authorize the President to exercise any function at his discretion, the Governor is authorized to exercise some discretion.*

One instance of a situation in which the Governor is not bound by the advice of the Council of Ministers would be when the Governor feels that a situation has arisen in which the government of the State cannot be carried on in accordance with the provisions of the Constitution. Obviously the Council of Ministers cannot be expected to give such a report to the Governor and the Governor has to exercise his discretion in the matter. Making a report to the President under Article 356 of the Constitution is one function of the Governor which has to be exercised under his discretion.*

It may be added that while the Governor has the power to dismiss an individual minister at any time, he can dismiss the Council of Ministers or the Chief Minister only when the Legislative assembly has expressed its lack of confidence in the Council of Ministers either by a vote of no confidence or censure.

The Governor cannot dismiss a Chief Minister on his subjective estimate. The strength of the Chief Minister has to be subjected to a vote in the Legislative assembly.

Very much like the Ministers in the Union, the Ministers in the States are collectively responsible to the Legislative assembly of the State. A person who is not a member of the Legislature can be appointed as a minister but such a minister has to become a member of Legislature within a period not exceeding six months.

---

* Article 163 (1) provides that there shall be a Council of Ministers to aid and advise the Governor in the exercise of his function, "except in so far as he is under the Constitution required to exercise his function or any of them in his discretion."

The Advocate General in the State has similar status as the Attorney General of India has at the Union level. Only a person who is qualified to be a Judge of the High Court can be appointed as Advocate General. He has the right to speak in the House but does not have the right to vote.

THE STATE LEGISLATURE

The Constitution provides for bicameral legislatures for certain states and unicameral legislatures for the rest. The question of organization of State Legislature in a single or two Houses has been left open.

Bicameral and Unicameral Legislatures

The Constitution prescribes that every State shall have a Legislative Assembly and the Governor, some States the Legislatures comprise two houses—The Legislative assembly and the Legislative Council.

The second house can be created or abolished by a simple procedure which does not involve any amendment of the Constitution. Apart from the resolution being passed by the Legislative assembly of the State passed by a majority of the total membership of the assembly not being less than two-thirds of the members actually present and voting followed by an Act of the parliament.*

The membership of the Council shall not be more than one third of the membership of the Assembly but not less than 40 (Article 171). The Council is partly elected (indirectly) and partly nominated. One sixth of the members of the Council are nominated by the Governor. The nominated categories are the persons having knowledge or practical experience in respect of matters such as literature, science art and social service etc.

The indirectly elected members make 5/6th of the total members of the Council. The voters include members of the local bodies, teachers and persons who are not members of the Assembly but are elected by members of the Legislative assembly.

The Legislative Council is not subject to dissolution. One third of the members retire on the expiry of every second year. The Council is thus a permanent body, only a fraction of its membership being changed every third year.

The Legislative Assembly

The Legislative assembly of each State is composed of members directly elected by the voters in the State. The number of members of the assembly is fixed at

---

* In 1957 a legislative Council; was created in Andhra Pradesh taking advantage of this provision but later *abolished by the same process.* West Bengal abolished the Legislative Council in 1969 and Punjab in 1960.

a minimum of 40 and maximum of 500, The only qualification prescribed for being eligible to election as member of a legislative assembly is that the citizen should be 25 years of age at the time of election.

The duration of the Legislative assembly is five years but may be dissolved sooner than five years by the Governor.

The minimum age in respect of members of the Legislative Council is 30 years.

*Legislative Procedure:*The Legislative procedure in a State Legislature with two chambers is almost identical to that in the Union Parliament. In case of Money Bills, the Council may retain it for a maximum period of 14 days. Even if some recommendations are made within this period, the Assembly is not obliged to accept any such recommendation.

In respect of other Bills, the Council can at best delay the Bill for a period not exceeding three months. In its second journey from the Assembly to the Council, the Bill can be withheld for not more than a month. Ultimately it is the will of the assembly that prevails

The Council as such acts as a brake to any hasty decision by the assembly. Being partly elected and partly nominated, the Council is only an advisory/ dilatory chamber.

At the State level there is no provision for a joint sitting of the two Houses as is the case at the Central level.

After a bill has been passed by the Legislature it goes to the Governor for his assent.

The Governor may assent, withhold assent or send the Bill back for reconsideration by the Legislature. It is obligatory for the Governor to reserve a Bill for consideration of the President if the Bill is so much derogatory to the powers of the High Court that it would endanger the Constitutional position of the High Court if the bill becomes law.

State of Jammu and Kashmir

The State of Jammu and Kashmir is one of the States of the Union of India and yet all the provisions relating to the States are not applicable to the state of Jammu and Kashmir,

The special status accorded to Jammu and Kashmir can be best understood by having a first hand knowledge of the background against which the former princely state became a part of the Indian Union.

Jammu and Kashmir was one of the princely States that had not sought accession to India till October 26, 1947 when it was attacked by Azad Kashmir Forces aided by the Pakistan armed forces. Maharaja Hari Singh executed an instrument of accession with the Government of India, like other princely states, and subsequently Jammu and Kashmir became a Part B State under the Union.

The State acceded to India under some very special circumstances. The Government of India, keeping in view those circumstances had decided that the jurisdiction of the Indian Union would be finally determined by the people of the State acting through their Constituent Assembly. This provision was introduced in the Indian Constitution under Article 370.

The Government of India had gone out of way to assure the people of Jammu and Kashmir that the constitutional relationship of the State with the Indian Union was subject to confirmation by the people of the State. However, this was misunderstood as a provision that over ruled the State's accession which was perfectly legal and in order. Pakistan has all along been insisting on taking advantage of this extra-legal assurance. Pakistan claims that the legal act of State's accession to India was still incomplete.

In the year 1954, the Constituent assembly of Jammu and Kashmir ratified the accession to India. On May 14, 1954, the President in consultation with the State Government made the Constitution (Application to Jammu and Kashmir) Order. Hereafter the jurisdiction of the Union extended to all Union subjects under the Constitution.

However, the provisions governing the Executive Legislative and Judiciary of the State were to be found in the Constitution drawn by the people of the State. The corresponding provisions of the Constitution of India were not applicable to the State of Jammu and Kashmir

The latest position is that the State of Jammu and Kashmir is an integral part of the Union of India. The territory of Jammu and Kashmir covered under the provisions of the Constitution of Jammu and Kashmir includes the territory presently under the occupation of Pakistan. The executive power of the State vests in the Governor who exercises the power with the advice of the Council of Ministers. The provisions with regard to the powers etc. of the Chief Minister are identical to those in other States of the Indian Union

In case of Jammu and Kashmir, the residual powers vest in the Legislature of that State except in matters relating to the prevention of activities relating to cession or secession or disrupting the sovereignty and integrity of India.

Parliament cannot make any law without the consent of the legislature where the State is to be affected by such legislation in respect of alterations in the name or territories of the State. Similarly no amendment of the Constitution of India shall extend to Jammu and Kashmir unless it is so extended by an Order of the President.

The Jurisdictions of the Comptroller and Auditor General, the Election Commission and the Special Leave Jurisdiction of the Supreme Court now stand extended to the State.

The provisions relating to Directive Principles of State Policy *do not* apply to the state of Jammu and Kashmir.

The Union government does not have powers to suspend the Constitution of the State on the ground of failure to comply with the directions given by the Union

In case of the State of Jammu and Kashmir, the federal relationship between the Union and the State gives more Rights to the State of Jammu and Kashmir than to other States in the Union.

Union Territories

The Constitution 7th Amendment Act of 1956 created a new category of States referred to as Union Territories to be administered by the Union.

Article 239 of the Constitution provides that every Union Territory shall be administered by the President acting to such an extent as he thinks fir through an Administrator to be appointed by him with such designation as he may specify.

Delhi is headed by a Lieutenant Governor. It has not been made a full fledged State. In other parts of the world, too, federal capitals like London and Paris are under a greater degree of central control over the administration of the cities. Similarly Washington and Canberra are under the Central government.

The Union Territories of Delhi and Pondicherry now have Legislative assemblies as well as a Council of Ministers. However, the Ministers in the Union Territories do not enjoy powers parallel to those of the Chief Ministers in States The Parliament has plenary powers of Legislation in case of the Union Territories.

HIGH COURTS

While the Constitution of India is federal in character, it has a single integrated system of judiciary that administers both the Union and the State laws. The Supreme Court stands at the apex of the system. The High Courts and a hierarchy of other courts exist at the District level The subordinates courts function under the control of the High Courts.

Article 214 of the Constitution of India provides that there shall be a High Court in each State. The parliament has, however, been given the powers to establish a common High Court for two or more States.

Judges of the High Court are appointed by the President in consultation with the Chief Justice of India, the Governor of the State (and also the Chief Justice of the concerned State)

There is no fixed minimum number of judges for the High Court. The number of judges is fixed by the President from time to time.*

Judges of the High Court appointed on a permanent basis serve up to the age of 62 years.

---

* Jammu and Kashmir High court has five judges while the number in case of Calcutta High Court is thirty-seven.

The prescribed qualification for appointment is that the person should be an Indian citizen with at least ten years of experience either as an advocate of a High Court or a judicial officer in the territory of India. The procedure for removal of a Judge of the High Court is similar to that prescribed in case of a judge of the Supreme Court.

The President has powers to transfer the judges of the High Court from one State to another. The power is exercised in consultation with the Chief Justice of India.

Besides judges appointed on a permanent basis there is a provision for the appointment of Judges as acting or additional judges. Additional judges have a term not exceeding two years. Acting judges are appointed when a permanent judge is away on leave or on some other duty.

The High Courts have been given full powers to make rules to regulate the business before them.

Jurisdiction

The Courts have the normal original and appellate jurisdiction. The criminal appellate jurisdiction extends to cases where the Session Judge or an additional Session Judge has awarded imprisonment exceeding seven years. The High Courts have the power to issue writs for the enforcement of Fundamental Rights. By giving this power to the High Courts (apart from the Supreme Court of India) these rights have been made more real for ordinary citizens

The courts exercise superintendence over all subordinate courts in the State. All types of Tribunals including the Election Tribunal operating within a State are subject to the superintendence of the High Courts. The tribunals enjoy quasi-judicial powers although they do not always follow the exact procedure adopted by the courts of justice. The superintendence on the part of the High Court is meant to ensure that these tribunals keep themselves within the limits of their jurisdiction and do not commit any acts amounting to gross miscarriage of justice.

The officers and servants of the High Court are appointed by the High Courts. The power of the Chief Justice of the High Court to appoint any member of the staff of the High Court also includes the power to dismiss any such member from the service of the court.

They also have the power to transfer to itself, from any subordinate court cases that may concern the interpretation of the Constitution.

The High Courts are empowered to issue writs similar to those that may be issued by the Supreme Court in these matters. The writs, however, are operative only within the territorial jurisdiction of the High Court.

Administrative Tribunals

Central Administrative Tribunals have been set up implementing the Article 323 A of the Constitution. The courts of law including the High Courts have since ceased to have jurisdiction to entertain any litigation relating to recruitment and other service matters relating to persons appointed by the public services of the Union.

Subordinate Courts

The Constitution of India incorporates detailed provisions concerning the judiciary at the subordinate level. These provisions ensure that the entire judicial system within the country functions independent of the executive—something contained in the Directive Principles of State Policy.

There are two categories of Subordinate Courts. Judges of the District Courts are appointed by the Governor in consultation with the High Court. Advocates and pleaders are appointed as judge of the District Court on the recommendation of the High Court but they must have been an advocate for a minimum period of seven years

Appointment of persons other than District judges are made by the Governor on the basis of open competition held by the State Public Services commission. The candidates who qualify and are appointed to the State Judicial service are given special training before posting. The persons so appointed also function under the superintendence of the High Court.*

The District Judge heads the hierarchy of judicial officers within the district.

1.9 FEDERALISM UNDER THE INDIAN CONSTITUTION

LEGISLATIVE AND EXECUTIVE POWERS OF UNION AND STATES

Even though the Indian Constitution has a strong unitary bias, the fact remains that the Constitution is based on a federal system in which all powers are divided between the Union and States with none of two enjoying sovereignty in the strict legal sense.

The Federal system in the Indian Constitution is one of its basic features. The Constitution divides all powers—legislative, executive and the States. Not withstanding a strong unitary bias, the Constitution of India is federal between the Union and the States. There is, however, a common judiciary. The States do not function as delegates of the Union. They are autonomous within their own spheres as laid down in the Constitution. All the same the Constitution has provided a number of devices through which the center can control the functioning of the States. The Constitution imposes limits for both the Union and the States and as such neither of the two can claim sovereignty in the

* A Subordinate Judge is sometimes vested also with powers of an Assistant Session Judge in which case he combines in his hands both civil and criminal powers like a District Judge.

strictly legal sense of the term. If the limitations imposed by the Constitution, in respect of legislative powers are violated, the Courts can declare such legislation as invalid.

Limitation with Respect to Territory and Subjects

The division of powers proceeds on two considerations. Each of the two, the Union and the States, function only within their defined territorial limits. Secondly, the jurisdiction of the Union and the States extends only with respect to the subjects allotted to them under the constitution.

The States can make laws that may be applicable to the entire State or a part of it but it has to be confined to its own territory.

Article 264(4) gives the Union powers to make laws that would be operative over the entire territory of India (including the States and Union territories). The Union laws even extend to persons and their property situated any where in the world. The State Legislatures, however, cannot claim the operation of any of their laws outside the boundaries of the State.

Distribution of Legislative Jurisdictions

The Government of India Act was the first to have provided a three fold distribution of legislative powers between the Union and the States. The three folds were the Federal, Provincial and the Concurrent. Schedule VII of the Indian Constitution contains three lists detailing the subjects of legislation.* List I or the Union List includes ninety nine subjects. It includes subjects like Defence, arms and ammunitions, atomic energy, foreign affairs, United Nations, declaration of war and treaties with foreign governments, citizenship, railways, airways, post and telegraph, telephones, wireless, currency and coinage, foreign trade, Reserve bank, insurance, mines minerals and oil resources, Survey of India, Census, Union Public Service Commission etc. Union Parliament has exclusive powers to legislate on the subjects included in the List I.

The State List contains sixty-one items. Some of the important subjects included in the State List include Law and Order and police, jails, public health and sanitation, agriculture, animal husbandry, intoxicating liquors, inter-state communications, local elections, State Public Service Commission, land revenue, taxes on vehicles etc.

The concurrent List has fifty-one items. The items included in this list are those for which uniformity through out the country is desirable but not essential. The List includes subjects like Education, Preventive detention in the interest of national security, marriage and divorce, adulteration of food stuffs, trade unions, social security, forests, labour welfare, price control, factories etc.

---

* The distribution does not apply to Union Territories, in regard to which Parliament is competent to legislate with respect to any subjects, including those that are enumerated in the State List.

The States are free to legislate on subjects included in the Concurrent List as long as there is no Union legislation on the subject. Once the Parliament enacts legislation on one particular subject, the State legislation in that area becomes subordinate to the Central laws.

An interesting situation would arise if a law passed by the State Legislature had been under consideration by the President and is later consented to by the President. In such a situation the State legislation would prevail over a Central law that might have been in operation earlier. Thus the States are given powers to pass a Legislation that may be more advanced than the Central legislation, already existing on the subject.

As regards the residuary powers, they are vested in the Union. The Center can pass legislations on subjects not included in any of the three lists. The Courts are to be the final authority for determining whether or not a subject falls under the residuary category.

Circumstances under which the Union Parliament Acquires Extended Powers

Union Parliament has powers to make laws on subjects included in the States List under exceptional circumstances.

While a Proclamation of Emergency made by the President is in operation, Parliament has powers to legislate with respect to State subjects.

It would be lawful for the Parliament to legislate on matters included in the State List in case two or more States resolve that the Parliament shall make laws on these subjects even though they fall within the State List. The Laws such passed shall, however, be operative only in the consenting States. Other States may, if they so desire adopt such legislations by passing a resolution to this effect in their own legislatures. Thus the jurisdiction of the Parliament can be extended by consent of the State legislatures.

The union Parliament can also pass legislations that are necessary for the implementation of international treaties even though such legislations may strictly be in the State's domain.

The powers of the Legislature of the State shall be exercised by the Parliament when Proclamation of Failure of Constitutional Machinery in the State has been issued by the President.

Distribution of Executive powers is mainly congruent with the distribution of legislative powers between the Union and the States. Thus while the executive powers of the State are limited to State territory, the Union has exclusive executive power over matters included in List 1.

On concurrent matters, the Constitution provides that the Union may, whenever it thinks fit, itself take up the administration of the Union laws relating to any concurrent subject. As a result of this provision, on concurrent subjects the executive power remains with the State with the following exceptions:

(i) Where a Law of the Parliament relating to such subject vests some executive function especially in the Union.
(ii) The executive power to implement any treaty or international agreement belongs exclusively to the Union whether the subject appertains to the Union, State or Concurrent List.
(iii) Where the matter concerns protection of railways within the State.
(iv) Executions of schemes essential to the welfare of the Scheduled castes and Scheduled Tribes in the States

In Emergencies The Union has powers to give directions relating to any matter so as to bring the State government under the complete control of the Union without suspending it. In the event of the failure of Constitutional machinery in a State, President is entitled to assume to himself all or any of the Executive powers of the State.

During the proclamation of a *financial emergency,* all Money Bills or financial Bills have to be reserved for the consideration of the President after they are passed by the State Legislature.

It is noteworthy that while it is not competent for the Union and a State to encroach upon each other's exclusive legislative jurisdiction by mutual consent, the Union may with the consent of a State entrust its own executive functions relating to any matter to such State government or its officers. Articles 258(1) and (A) provide that the State too can entrust any of its executive functions to the Union with mutual consent.

The Union government can authorize to delegate its duties to a State Government irrespective of the consent of the State government under Art. 258(2) of the Constitution.

A study of administrative relations between the Union and the States must take into account the provisions contained in Art 262 which deal with the waters of inter-state rivers and river valleys. The parliament may, by law, provide for adjudication of any dispute with respect to the use, distribution or control of the waters of any inter-state rivers or river valley.

Indian Federation is unique in many ways. Apart from the distribution of Legislative and Executive powers referred to above, there are certain features that are typical of the Indian system.

Unlike USA, where the States have their own Constitution separate from that of the Union, the States of the India Union have a uniform Constitution.

The States in USA and Australia have their own judicial systems unrelated to the Federal judiciary. In India the Supreme Court and the High Courts in State function under a common judicial system.

While the Governors head the Executive in the States, they are appointed by the Union government (President).

Key administrative positions in the States are manned by personnel of the All India services.

The organization of the Comptroller and Auditor General is concerned with the audit of the accounts of both the Union and the State governments. The organization is managed by the officers of the Indian Audit and Accounts Service.

Both at the level of the Union and the States elections are conducted by the Election Commission of India appointed by the President.

Planning Commission, created by the center, directs and regulates the entire socio-economic activity on a national basis.

ALLOCATION OF RESOURCES BETWEEN UNION AND STATES

> *Realizing the limitations on the financial resources of the States, and the growing needs of the community in a welfare State, the Constitution has made specific provisions empowering the Parliament to set aside a portion of its revenues for the benefits of the States, not in stated proportions but according to their needs. The resources of the Union government are not meant exclusively for the benefit of Union activities.*
>
> —Supreme Court

The Constitution of India makes elaborate provisions with respect to the relationship between the Union and the States in the field of financial allocation of resources.

The distribution of tax-revenue between the Union and the States stands as follows:

(a) Taxes belonging exclusively to the Union: Union sources include Corporation Tax, Custom duties, Excise duties on tobacco and certain other goods manufactured in India, Estate duty, Railways, Reserve bank of India, Taxes on income other than agricultural incomes etc. (20 items)

(b) Taxes belonging exclusively to the States: Excise duty on alcoholic products and opium etc, land revenue, taxes on lands and buildings, taxes on vehicles, entertainment taxes, receipts from fees in respect of matters in the State list, stamp duties in respect of documents etc. (20 items)

(c) Taxes levied and collected by the Union but assigned to the States: Estate duty in respect of property other than agricultural land, taxes on the sale purchase of newspapers and on advertisements published therein, taxes other than stamp duties on transactions in stock exchanges and future markets etc. (7 items)

(d) Duties levied by the Union but collected and appropriated by the States: Stamp duties and duties of excise on medicinal and toilet preparations.

(e) Taxes levied and collected by the Union but which may be distributed between the Union and the States: taxes on income other than agricultural income.

The Constitution also provides for grants-in aid by the Union to such States as parliament may determine to be in need of assistance particularly for the promotion of welfare of tribal areas or raising the level of administration of the Scheduled areas.

Constitution and Functions of the Finance Commission

It is constitutionally obligatory on the part of the President to appoint Finance Commission at stated intervals to recommend measures relating to the distribution of financial resources between the Union and the States. (Example—per centage of net proceeds of income tax which should be assigned by the Union to the States) The Constitutional provisions in this regard are contained in Art. 280 of the Constitution.

The Finance Commission makes recommendations to the President as to:

(i) The distribution between the Union and the States of the net proceeds of taxes (like income tax) and the allocation between the States of the respective share of such proceeds. The parliament is not directly involved with the assignment and distribution of income tax proceeds levied and collected by the Union government.

(ii) The principles which should govern the grant-in-aid to the States.

The eleventh Finance Commission was appointed in 2002. The Commission acts as a bridge between the Union and the States. While on the one hand the Commission takes into consideration the cases of needy States, it insulates Union government from political pressure that may be applied by States to corner a greater share from out of the Central kitty.

Financial Control by the Union and Emergency: Art 354 authorizes the President to direct that, for a period not exceeding beyond the expiration of the financial year in which the Proclamation of Emergency ceases to operate, all or any of the provisions relating to the division of taxes between the Union and the States and grants in aid shall be suspended

Borrowing Powers of the Union and the States

Wile the Union of India has unlimited powers to borrow on the security of the revenues of India both within India and outside, the Constitution has set a number of constitutional limitations on the borrowing power of a State.

The States cannot borrow outside India. The State Executive can borrow within the territory of India upon the security of the revenues of the State subject to certain conditions.

The Government of India may itself offer a loan to a State under a Law made by the Parliament. No fresh loan can be raised by the State so long such a loan remains unpaid.

Demand for more Financial Powers by States

The States continue to argue that the Center has allocated to itself high revenue yielding subjects while the responsibility for implementing welfare schemes like education, health lie with the State governments. Prime minister Morarji

Desai resisted such demands during his tenure. Mrs. Indira Gandhi was also of the opinion that no amendment to the Constitution in this respect was necessary.*

FEDERALISM AND EMERGENCY PRIOVISIONS

The Supreme Court has asserted the competence of the Court to review the justification or otherwise of every case of proclamation of Emergency in the States which has made the Union government realize that judicial intervention might declare invalid a declaration of emergency if imposed without adequate justification. This assertion has come as a very healthy development in retaining the Federal spirit of our Constitution.

References to Emergency have been made in the preceding chapters more than once. The provision of Emergency powers to the Center has been a subject of criticism right from the days of the Constituent assembly debates.**

Does the provision for Emergency concentrate too much power in the Union which is likely to destroy the federal character of the Constitution? For a proper analysis of this criticism, let us first examine the conditions under which the Constitution allows imposition of Emergency.

Categories of Emergency

(a) If the President is satisfied that a grave emergency exists whereby the security of India or any part of its territory is threatened by war, external aggression or armed rebellion, he may proclaim a state of emergency.

As soon as an emergency is declared, the Federal provisions of the Constitution cease to operate in the area affected by the proclamation. The Executive power of the Union here after extends to the giving of any directions to any State Executive in the emergency area.

Parliament's law making powers extend to the subjects enumerated in the State's list. The federal government literally becomes a unitary government.

(b) *Constitutional Emergency in States* can be proclaimed if the President is satisfied on receipt of a report from the State Governor that a situation has arisen in which the government of the State cannot be carried on in accordance with the Constitutional provisions. In such a situation the President may assume

---

* "No amendment to the Constitution is necessary to alter the relations between the Centre and States on the ground that the financial deficiencies of particular States are being periodically examined and provided for by the Finance Commission by making larger grants to those States from the Union revenues, according to the provisions of the Constitution."

** "Looking at all the provisions and scrutinizing the powers that have been given in almost every article, it seems to me, the name only of liberty or democracy will remain under the Constitution." K.T. Shah

for himself all powers in respect of all or any function of the State or he may vest these powers on the Governor or on any other Executive authority. The one exception is that the President cannot assume the powers vested in the High Court.

The Parliament may pass all legislative enactments for the State including financial legislations in such a situation. Any law made by competent authority continues in force until repealed or altered by a competent authority or legislature.

During the period of emergency, due to war or break down of constitutional machinery in the State, the Fundamental Rights remain suspended. Virtually the whole chapter on Fundamental Rights can be suspended during the operation of emergency. However such orders have to be put up before the Parliament for approval, as soon as possible.

(c) Article 360 of the Constitution provides for declaration of a financial emergency. During a financial emergency, the executive authority of the Union extends to the giving of directions to any State or observe such canons of financial propriety as may be specified in the direction. The directions may include: requiring the reduction of salaries and allowances of government servants including Judges of the High Courts and the Supreme Court.

In December 1978 the Constitution Forty Fifth amendment was adopted by the Parliament. The amendment ensures that the proclamation of emergency can be made only on the basis of written advice tendered to the President by the cabinet. Emergency can be proclaimed only when the security of the country is threatened by war, external aggression or armed rebellion (Internal disturbance short of armed rebellion cannot be a ground for the imposition of Emergency). The declaration of Emergency has to be approved by the Parliament within one month and that too by a majority of the total membership and not less than two thirds of the members present and voting.

1.10 PUBLIC SERVICES AND PUBLIC SERVICE COMMISSIONS

Members of the public services hold office during the pleasure of the President or the Governor. Article 311 however ensures that no member of the public services can be dismissed by the President or the Governor, arbitrarily. No member of the civil service can be dismissed or removed by an authority subordinate to that by which he was appointed. The civil servant has to be given a reasonable opportunity for showing cause against the action proposed to be taken against him.

Under the parliamentary system of government, while the elected representatives lay down the policy of administration, a large body of officials carry out the actual administration with no concern with politics. The ministers form the political executive that keeps on changing while the public servants are appointed by a different procedure and have no political connection. The ministers continue in office as long as they enjoy majority support in the legislature and lose office as soon as the Ministry is dissolved. On the other hand, the permanent executive continues.

The executive officials are experts in the functioning of the government. The Ministers cannot always claim such expertise in the portfolio they may be heading.

The political executive has to be sensitive and responsive to fresh ideas. Civil services, on the other hand tend to be more tied to rules and precedents. All the same, civil services are an essential part of Parliamentary form of government all over the world.

The Constitution has made specific provisions to ensure that civil servants are recruited by procedures that ensure their political neutrality and efficiency. These measures attract the best talent to public services. They are offered reasonable security against arbitrary action by their superiors including Ministers but make them answerable to Courts of Law and such discipline as may be prescribed under the Conduct Rules.

Tenure of Office

The Constitution explicitly maintains that officials, both civil and military, hold office during the pleasure of the President or the Governor. Literally this means that a government employee can be dismissed or removed from service any time and on any ground. In practice the dismissal is subject to certain constitutional safe guards.

So far Government servants engaged on a contract basis are concerned, compensation is payable in cases of premature termination if such a condition exists in the contract.

Safeguards for Civil Servants

A civil servant shall not be dismissed or removed from service by any authority subordinate to that by which he was appointed This provision insulates public servants from the caprices of officers of junior ranks.

The civil servant has to be given reasonable opportunity of being heard in respect of the charges brought against him.

The punishing authority is required to frame specific charges against the delinquent official. The charges have to be intimated to the government servant concerened. He must be given an opportunity to answer those charges and after considering his answers, take its decision. The rules of natural justice should be observed in coming to the findings against the accused official.

Exceptions

The 2nd provison to article 11(2) provides that where the President or the Governor is satisfied that in the interest of the security of the State, it is not expedient to hold such enquiry a person holding a civil post may be dismissed removed or reduced in rank.*

Yet another exception is where a person is dismissed or removed or reduced in rank on the ground of conduct which has led to his conviction on a criminal charge.

If the authority empowered to dismiss or remove a person or to reduce him in rank is satisfied that for some reason to be recorded by that authority in writing that it is not reasonably practicable to hold such an inquiry, no inquiry need be held and no opportunity need be given.

Administrative Tribunals Act 1985

The Constitution Amendment Act, 1976 inserted into the Art. 323 A has taken out the adjudication of disputes relating to the recruitment and conditions of service of the public services of the Union and the States from the hands of Civil Courts and the High Courts and to place it before an Administrative Tribunal for the Union or of a State (as the case may be).

The Central Administrative Tribunal now adjucates disputes and complaints with respect to recruitment and conditions of service of persons appointed to public services and posts in connection with the affairs of the Union excepting:

(i) Members of the Defence Forces.

(ii) Officers and servants of the Supreme Court or of any High Court.

(iii) Members of the secretarial staff of the Parliament or of any legislature of any State or Union Territory.

The only court to which a person aggrieved by the decision of the Administrative Tribunal can approach is the Supreme Court. The High Court is not competent to interfere.

Public Service Commissions

The Constitution provides that there shall be a Public Service Commission for the Union, and a Public Service Commission for each State or a Joint Public Service Commission for a group of States if the Union Parliament provides for the establishment of such a Joint Public Service Commission,. in pursuance of a resolution to that effect being passed by the concerned State Legislatures.

The number of members of the Commission and the conditions of their service shall be determined by the President in case of the Union Public Service Commission and by the Governor of the State in case of a State Commission.

---

* Union of India vs. Tulsiram AIR 1985 SC 1416 (para 70).

The conditions of service of a member of the Commission cannot be altered to his/her disadvantage after appointment.

Appointment and Terms of Office of Members

The appointment of the Chairman and members of the Commission shall be made by the President in case of Union Public Service Commission and by the Governor of the State in case of a State Commission.

Half of the members of the Commission have to be from amongst those who have held office under the Government of India or of a State for at least 10 years.*

The term of service of a member of a Commission shall be six years from the date of his entering upon office or until he attains the age of 65 in the case of Union Commission or of 62 years in the case of a State or Joint Commission.

A member's ofice tenure can be terminated by resignation or removal if the member is adjudged insolvent or engages himself during his term in paid employment outside the duties of his office or adjudged as infirm in mind or body by the President.

Even on the case of State Commission, only the President is empowered to make a reference to the Supreme Court for alleged misbehaviour on the part of member of the Commission which can lead to his removal.

Independence of the Commission

The Constitution seeks to maintain the independence of the Public Service Commission in several ways:

(i) The Chairperson or a Member of the Commission can be removed from office only in the manner and for the grounds specified in the Constitution.

(ii) Art. 318 provides that the conditions of service of a member cannot be changed to his disadvantage after appointment.

(iii) The expenses of the Commission are charged on the Consolidated Fund of India or of the State as the case may be.

On ceasing to hold office the Chairman and the members are subject to certain disabilities with respect to future employment.

(i) The Chairman of the UPSC is ineligible for further employment under the Government of India or under the Government of a State.

(ii) The Chairman of the State Public Service Commission shall be eligible for employment as the Chairman or any other member of the UPSC or the Chairman of any other State Commission but not eligible for any other employment under the Union or the State government.

---

* Article 316.

Functions of the Public Services Commissions

The Commissions are advisory bodies. The appointments are made by the respective Union or State governments.

The functions performed by the Commission include:

(i) To advise on any matter so referred to them by the President or the Governor. The consultation prescribed by the Constitution is to afford proper assistance to the government in the matter of assessing the guilt of a delinquent officer. However it has been held by the Supreme Court that if the government fails to consult the Commission, the resulting act of the government is not invalidated for reason of such omission.

(ii) To conduct examinations for appointments to services of the Union and the Services of the respective States.

(iii) To exercise such additional functions as may be provided for by an Act of Parliament or the Legislature iof a State in respect of the services and also in respect of services of any local authority or corporation constituted by law or of any public institution.

(iv) The Commission (both the UPSC and the States Commissions) are to be consulted on all matters relating to methods of recruitment to civil services and civil posts. Similar consultation is a statutory provision with respect to all disciplinary matters affecting a person serving under the Government of India or of the Government of a State.

The Constitution provides that the President or the Governor has powers to specify the matters in which either generally or in any particular class of cases it shall not be necessary for a Public Service Commission to be considered,. But all such regulations must be laid before the appropriate Legislature.

Report of the Public Service Commissions

It is the duty of the Public Service Commissions to present annually to the President a report as to the work done by the Commission and explaining where the advice of the Commission was not accepted and the reasons why the recommendations were not accepted. The report is to be laid before the House of Parliament. The State Commissions similarly submit report to the Governor and the latter has a duty to lay the same before the Legislatures.

How Far is the Commission's Advice Binding on the Government?

The Constitution has no provision that would make makes it obligatory on the part of the Government to act upon the advice of the Commission. The only obligation on the part of the government is to state the Legislature the reasons for non-acceptance of the Commission's advice.

All India Services

Officers of the All India Services (like the IAS and the IPS) are appointed and controlled by the Union government. Art. 312 of the Constitution authorizes the Union government to include in the category of All India Services such services in the prescribed manner. The Union government exercises control over the functioning of the State governments by appointing these officers to key positions in the States.

Rights of Civil Servants

Every public servant possesses the Fundamental Rights guaranteed under the Constitution to all citizens. Under provisions of Art. 309, the State has been given the powers to regulate the conditions of service of public servants. The State has constitutional powers to regulate the conditions of service of public servants. Such regulations are, however, permissible only to the extent it is necessary in the interest of efficiency, integrity, impartiality, discipline and responsibility which have a direct proximate and rational relation to the conditions of public service as well as based on general grounds like public order.

1.11 OFFICIAL LANGUAGE

No less than 1,652 spoken languages, including 63-non-Indian languages, are current in the sub-continent The makers of the Constitution had, therefore, to select some of these languages as the recognized medium of official communication in order to save the country from total linguistic anarchy. Hindi, including its kindred variants, was found to claim 46 per cent of usage and was as such picked up as the official language of the Union; subject to continuation of English for the same purpose for a limited period of 15 years.

The provisions relating to the Official Language of the Union are contained in Articles 343-351 of the Constitution.

The Constituent Assembly had witnessed some very emotionally charged debates during the consideration of the Official Language. The compromise formula provided that the official language of the Union shall be Hindi written Devnagari script and also that English language will continue to be used for a period of fifteen years from the commencement of the Constitution. Union Parliament was authorized to provide for the continued use of English after fifteen years for any specific purpose.

Inter-State Communications

The Constitution provides that the language for the time being authorized for use in the Union for official purposes (English) shall be the official language of communication between one State and another State and between a State and the Union. If, however, two or more States agree that Hindi language should be the official language for communication between such States, that language may be used for such communication instead of English.*

Status of Regional Languages

Article 345 of the Constitution empowers every State Legislature to adopt any one or more languages for use in the State for all or any official purposes of the concerned State. However, with a view to prevent any language fanaticism, the President has been given powers to direct a State government to recognize a particular language for official purposes either for the whole or a part of the State. If a substantial proportion of the population of a State so desires it can make a representation to the President in this regard.

1.12 ELECTIONS

Article 327 empowers the Union Parliament to make laws relating to all matters in connection with elections to the Houses of the Parliament and the Houses of Legislature of a State. In respect of matters not covered by legislation by Parliament, the State legislatures have been given subsidiary powers.

The Constitution lays down the procedure for election of the President and the Vice-President. The Representation of People Acts, along with Delimitation Commission Acts, govern the procedure for election and the formation and delimitation of the constituencies relating to election.

The Constitution provides certain principles with regard to elections. There has to be one electoral roll for every territorial constituency. No person shall be excluded from the electoral roll on the grounds only of religion, race, caste, sex or any of them.**

The elections have to be held on the basis of adult suffrage. The only disqualification is with respect to persons who are less than 18 years of age, of unsound mind or convicted for crime or any corrupt or illegal practice.

While the system of proportional representation has been adopted for elections to the office of the President and the Vice-President, the system has not been adopted for election to the Legislature of the Union or the States.

Election Commission

The Constitution, vide Article 324, provides for Election Commission as an independent body to supervise the entire procedure and machinery for elections and for othetr ancillary purposes The Commission acts as a body independent

* Article 346.

** Article 325. There is no provision for communal, separate or special representation.

of executive control and thus ensures elections free from the control of the party that may be in power when elections to the new Legislatures take place.

The Election Commission comprises a Chief Election Commissioner and such other Commissioners as the President may from time to time fix.*

The Election Commission deals with the following matters related to the conduct and supervision of elections.

(i) Election of the President and the Vice-President.

(ii) The Union Parliament and the composition of its two Chambers.

(iii) Composition of State Legislatures.

(iv) Elections to Parliament and State Legislatures.

(v) Reservation of seats in the House of the People and State Assemblies for Scheduled Castes and Scheduled Tribes.

(vi) Determination of popul;ation for election purposes.

The Chief Election Commissioner can only be removed by each House of Parliament, by a special majority and on the ground of proved misbehaviour or incapacity. Other Election Commissioners can be removed only on the recommendation of the Chief Election Commissioner.

The Election Commission has been given powers under the Constitution to supervise and conduct all elections to Parliament and State Legislatures and also election to the offices of the President and the Vice-President.

Regional Commissioners are appointed by the President in consultation with the Election Commission on the eve of a general election to the House of the People or to the State Legislatures to assist the Election Commission.

The Conduct of Elections

The process starts with the updating of electoral rolls. The machinery consists of the Election Commission, the Chief Electoral Officer and the Electoral Registration Officer of the respective constituencies. It is the responsibility of the Electoral Registration Officer, appointed for the State Assembly, constituency to prepare and annually revise the electoral roll for the constituency. The Electoral Registration Officer is assisted by Assistant Electoral Registration Officer in the performance of the functions assigned to him.

The actual poll is conducted by a large number of Presiding and Polling Officers. For every polling station, a presiding officer and a few polling officers are appointed.

The polling arrangements involve a large number of policemen, Magistrates and other officers appointed as Supervisors by the Election Commission.

Article 324(2).

ABOLITION OF SEPARATE ELECTORATES AND RESERVATION

The Constitution makes exception with regard to reservation of seats only in respect of Scheduled Castes, Scheduled Tribes and Anglo-Indians.

The President under Article 331 is empowered to nominate a maximum of two members of the Anglo-Indian community to the House of the People if he is satisfied that the community is not adequately represented. The case for nomination would arise if no Anglo-Indian has been elected to the House of the People in the General election.

The same applies to States where the Governor is empowered to nominate such members to the State Legislative Assembly as he may consider appropriate if in his opinion the community needs representation and has not been adequately represented. The community has been given representation in all Staes where the population of the community exceeds two thousand. Presently Anglo-Indians find representation in the State assemblies of West Bengal, Andhra Pradesh, Bihar, Maharashtra, Kerala, Madhya Pradesh, Tamil Nadu, Karnataka and Uttar Pradesh.

Parts of the Constitution Unamendable

There have been two very important judgments of the Supreme Court with regard to the power of the Parliament to amend the Constitution. In the Golak Nath case, it was held that Fundamental Rights cannot be amended and that if any such amendment was to be undertaken, a new Constituent Assembly must be convened. The Parliament sought to supersede the judgment by passing the Constitution 24th Amendment Act whereby it was provided that the validity of a Constitution Amendment Act shall not be open to question on the ground that it takes away or affects a Fundamental Right. Later the validity of the 24th Constitution Amendment Act was challenged in the Keshavananad vs. State of Kerala case in the Supreme Court. The validity of the 24th Amendment was upheld.

The Supreme court, however, asserted that there are certain basic features of the Constitution of India which cannot be altered in exercise of the powers under Art. 368. These basic features are sovereignty and territorial integrity of India, the federal system, judicial review and Parliamentary system of government

Judicial innovation has thus introduced the doctrine of basic features into the Constitution.

Consolidated Fund of India

Article 114 of the Constitution provides that no amendment to the Finance Bill shall be proposed in either House of the Parliament which will have the effect of varying the amount or altering the destination of any grant so made or varying the amount of expenditure charged on the Consolidated Fund. The salaries and expenditure relating to the office of the President, Vice-President Speaker and Deputy Speaker of the House of People, Judges of the Supreme Court and the High Courts, Comptroller and Auditor General etc. are thus protected from a vote in the Parliament.

When is discrimination permissible? Discrimination is not unconstitutional when practiced on considerations other than religion, race, caste, sex, place of birth or any of them. A law making women ineligible for jobs inside the mines would not be unconstitutional since it is based on consideration of safety and not on ground of sex. The State can make special provisions for women and children or advancement of any socially and educationally backward class of citizens. Such affirmative actions would not be deemed as discriminatory.

2

Constitutional Provisions and Education in India

The State shall strive to provide within ten years from the commencement of the Constitution, free and compulsory education to all children up to the age of 14.

2.1 DIRECTIVE PRINCIPLES OF STATE POLICY

(By a Constitution amendment the State's liability has been restricted to children between 6-14 years of age)

Article 15 of the Constitution had provided that "the *State shall not discriminate against any citizen on grounds* only *of religion, race, caste, sex, and place of birth or any of them"*. An exception however was provided in respect of women and children. The State was permitted to make special provisions for these two categories of citizens.

In 1951 the First Amendment to the Constitution further enlarged the scope for exceptions. The State was allowed to make any special provision for advancement of any socially and educationally backward class of citizens or for the Scheduled Castes and Scheduled Tribes.

By the 93rd Amendment of January 20, 2006, Article 15(5) was inserted which reads as follows: "Nothing in this article or in sub-clause (g) of clause (i) of article 19 shall prevent the State4 from making any special provision by law, for the advancement of any socially and educationally backward classes of citizens or for the Scheduled castes and the Scheduled Tribes in so far as such special provision relate to their admission to educational institutions including private educational institutions whether aided or unaided by the State, other than the minority educational institutions referred to in clause (1) of Article 30.

The scope of this Article is very wide. The prohibition is leveled not only against the State but also against individuals in as much as discrimination cannot be practiced even in respect to individually owned shops, public restaurants, hotels and places of public entertainment. It obviously includes educational institutions that are made open to public. even if they are being run by individuals and not accepting any grants from the State.

While going through the text of Article 15, the use of word 'only' needs special attention. The significance of the word only is that if there is any other ground or consideration for the differential treatment besides those prohibited by this Article, the discrimination will not be unconstitutional. Thus discrimination in favour of women cannot be challenged in a profession like nursing. If an employer insists on employing only males for a job that requires high level of physical strength, the discrimination cannot be regarded as unconstitutional.

The Indian Air Force does not employ women as pilots on fighter planes. They are also not eligible in combat regiments. These are examples of discriminations that cannot be challenged as being unconstitutional. The prohibition in these cases is not only sex based but is based on the specific requirements of the particular jobs.

In India there are schools exclusively for girls. This is again a case where the discrimination cannot be considered as unconstitutional. The classification as Boys school and Girls school is not just sex based but is enforced to meet specific demands of the community being served.

Fee concessions and Scholarships in schools to students belonging to Scheduled Castes and Scheduled Tribes are also examples of discriminations that cannot be challenged. since they are meant for the advancement of an educationally backward group of citizens. In some States, Girls schools provide transport facilities to students residing far way from the school free or at highly subsidized costs. Male students cannot claim similar facilities under equal rights because these exceptions are already covered under Article 15 of the Constitution.

Similarly it is permissible for the State to reserve seats for members of the Scheduled castes, Scheduled Tribes and Other backward Classes in public as well as private institutions. The institutions however can determine the qualifications for entry or admission and these cannot be challenged unless it can be proved that such qualifications have been framed with the ulterior motive of keeping the S/C, S/T or the OBC population out.

Article 19 gives all Indian citizens the freedom *"to practice any profession or to carry on any occupation, trade or business"*.

No State or society running or managing an educational institution can debar a person from being employed in any school on grounds of caste as long as he has the other requisite qualifications. In State run schools reservation based on caste is permissible in respect of Scheduled caste/Scheduled Tribe candidates. It is now being insisted that similar reservations must also be available in the private sector.

All the same no person can claim to be exempted from minimum qualifications laid down for a particular job or profession on the plea that he belongs to SC/ST/OBC or any other class for which exceptions have been provided for in the Constitution.

" Nothing of the said clause shall affect the operation of an existing law in so far it imposes or prevent the State from making any law imposing, in the interests of general public, reasonable restrictions on the exercise of the rights conferred by the said sub-clause and in particular nothing in the sub-clause shall affect the operation of any existing law in so far as it relates to or to prevent the State from making any law relating to

(i) The professional or technical qualifications necessary for practicing any profession or carrying on any occupation, trade or business or

(ii) The carrying on by the State, or by a Corporation owned or controlled by the State of any trade, business, industry or service whether to the exclusion, complete or partial of citizens or other wise."

As a typical example the decision of the State in prescribing B.Ed or an equivalent professional qualification as essential for a teaching job cannot be challenged on the grounds that it adversely affects candidates from S/T since facilities for acquiring such educational qualifications do not exist where these tribes normally reside.

It may be a hypothetical situation but the law provides that the State can exclude private citizens from opening schools in a particular region. But in such a case the private citizens have to be given an opportunity to be heard as to why they want to open a school in that region even when there are enough State run schools already existing. The requirement of an *essentiality certificate* from the Education Officer of that particular region for opening a new private run school cannot be deemed unconstitutional.

Article 26; *"Subject to public order, morality and health, every religious denomination or any section thereof shall have the right (a) to establish and maintain institutions for religious and charitable purposes."* The Article also guarantees the freedom to every religious denomination to own and acquire moveable and immoveable property and administer such property in accordance with law.

The religious institutions however are subject to such laws as may have been framed to maintain law and order and the security and integrity of the State. Madarsas and Gurukuls are free to impart religious education as long as it does not in any way promote hatred between different groups of citizens or endangers the security of the State.

Article 28 Under provisions of this Article neither the State nor any other body can impart religious instruction in any school wholly maintained by State funds. However institutions established under any endowment or trust which requires that religious instruction be imparted in such institution are exempted from this prohibition. This exemption is valid even when such an institution is being administered by the State.

In respect of State recognized and grant aided schools, it is provided that no person attending such institutions can be compelled to take part in any religious instruction without parental consent.

The implications arising out of these checks are that while institutions run by minorities are eligible for grant in aid from the State, religious instruction in such schools can be imparted only to such students as are willing to attend religious instruction classes. Denominational schools can maintain their religious character but without forcing religious instruction on any unwilling student.

Article 29 guarantees certain educational rights to groups of Indian citizens having a distinct language, script or culture of its own. The article provides for the conservation of cultural diversity within the country. This article gives the term minority a very wide connotation. Religion alone is not the only criteria for determining that a certain group comprises a minority. Minority is recognized also on the basis of language, script or culture. *"No citizen shall be denied admission into any educational institution maintained by the State funds on ground only of religion, race, caste language or any of them."*

The Article embodies a very important principle. Every Indian citizen has the freedom to chose any educational institution maintained by the State or receiving government aid. Apart from guaranteeing the fundamental right of an individual citizen, it also protects the language, script or culture of a section of Indian people.

The right to admission cannot be denied to any citizen only on the basis of religion, race, caste, language or any of them. However if a person is denied admission because he does not have the requisite academic qualifications, he cannot complain that his fundamental right has been violated. A breach of fundamental rise would arise only if he has the academic qualification required but admission has been refused because he belongs to a certain religion, race or caste.

Here again one should not lose sight of the word *only* in the Article. If a State is maintaining a chain of Government schools, it can certainly have an admission plan according to which specific schools would admit students coming from feeder schools according to a pre-determined plan. A student can be denied admission because his feeder school has been attached to some other State school. Since the refusal at any particular school in such a case is not based on religion, race or caste it cannot be challenged as violating a fundamental right.

Article 30 gives the religious minorities the right to establish and administer educational institutions of its choice. The State, in granting aid to educational institutions shall not discriminate against educational institutions managed by a religious community.

If the property of a minority educational institution has to be acquired, the State has to pay full compensation

It has to be appreciated that the Article does not say that minorities should establish educational institutions only for religious teaching. Similarly linguistic minorities do not have to establish schools that would teach only their language. The religious and linguistic minorities have the right to establish schools of their choice. But such institution must also provide general and secular education so that the students who pass from such schools are no less eligible for admission to institutes of higher learning.

Yet another important thing to be noted is that the right to administer does not include the right to mal-administer. The State providing grant in aid is as such within its rights to prescribe reasonable regulations to ensure that the institution is run efficiently and in accordance with the ruled for grant in aid.

The protection of minority status is available to institutions established by the minority both before and after the commencement of the Constitution.

Article 30 does not give the majority the right to establish and administer educational institutions of their choice. As the Constitution does not precisely define the term minority, groups like Janis within the Hindu Community have started claiming minority status.

The term linguistic minority has been interpreted by the Supreme Court to mean a group of people who are in a numerical minority in a State as whole.

Indian Constitution is not an instrument for furtherance of the culture and language of the majority community alone. Minorities have been given adequate protection to preserve their religious beliefs and cultural institutions. By doing so we have averted situation as it prevails in Sri Lanka where a frustrated minority is fighting armed battles against the government asking for a separate State.

The Rights under Article 30 cast a special responsibility on minority communities.

They should not remain isolated from the mainstream of national life. Indian society by tradition is fragmented and as the country progresses there is need for greater social cohesion. Educational and cultural institutions irrespective of who is maintaining them have to become agents of social change. Nothing could be more unfortunate than their perpetuating barriers between different groups of Indian citizens.

In the arena of competitive politics, there is always the danger of the minority always clamoring for more than what the secular constitution offers. The very foundations of Independence would be imperiled if minorities were to revert to the pre-independence vortex of separatism and communalism. Secularism itself would be violated if the government were to suppress the legal rights of the majority just to garner votes from the minority community. The confidence of majority is no less important for national unity and strength than minority rights.

2.2 THE RIGHTS OF CHILDREN TO FREE AND COMPULSORY EDUCATION ACT, 2009

Background

With a view to specially implement the provisions contained in Article 45 of the

Constitution, the government of India, the State Governments and the Union Territories took a number of steps for providing free and compulsory universal elementary education to all children between the age group 6 to 14 years. In 2002, a new Article 21A inserted in the constitution. As a follow up of this article, the government of India decided to introduce the 'Right to Education Bill in 2005. However, it could be introduced in the Parliament in the year 2008.

The Right of children for free and compulsory education Bill having been passed by both Houses of parliament received the assent of the president on 26th August 2009. It came in the Statue Book as 'The Rights Of Children To Free And Compulsory Education Act 2009 (35 of 2009)'.

2.3 SIGNIFICANCE OF THE ACT

In several educational quarters the Education Act has been hailed as a great landmark legislation in the history of education in India. It is expected that its implementation will provide not only for free and compulsory education to every child between the age of 6 and 14 years of age but also help in raising standard of education. However, there are sceptics who do not find any weight in such arguments. It is true that the Act has raised high hopes but if past performance in free and compulsory education is any indicator it does not inspire much.

As a matter of fact every state has its own Education Act/Code which includes almost all these provisions in the present Act. Nevertheless there is one major difference. Now it is backed by an Act of the Parliament. The Present Act specifies the duties of various stake holders in education i.e., the Central Government, the State Government, Local Authorities, the Parents and Teachers etc.

It appears a detailed mechanism will have to be worked out to demarc clearly the role of various authorities. From the contents of the Act, one is inclined to get the impression, that it will lead to more litigation and may become a haven for the legal community.

The Act comprising seven chapters specifies the rights of the child as also the duties of various agencies involved in the imparting of education to the child.

2.4 MAIN PROVISIONS OF THE ACT

- Provision of free and compulsory elementary education (class I to VIII) to every child.
- Ensuring availability of a neighbourhood school.
- Ensuring that the children belonging to weaker section are not discriminated against and prevented from pursuing and completing elementary education on any grounds;
- Providing infrastructure including school building, teaching staff and learning equipment;
- Providing special training facility.
- Ensuring and monitoring admission, attendance and completion of elementary education by every child;

- Ensuring good quality elementary education conforming to the standards and norms specified in the Schedule; (given separately).
- Ensuring timely prescribing of curriculum and courses of study for elementary education; and
- Providing training facility for teachers.
- Charging of no capitation fee.
- No screening procedure for admission.
- No denial for admission.
- No holding back in the same class.
- No expulsion.
- No physical punishment to the child.
- No mental harassment of the child.
- Appropriate condition of service teachers.
- Constitute of Managing Committee for every school committee.
- Suitable pupils teachers ratio.
- Filling of vacancy of teachers in time.
- Prohibition of deployment of teachers for non-education purposes.
- Prohibition of tuition by teachers.
- Monitoring child's right to education.
- Updating of curriculum from time to time and continuous and comprehensive evaluation.
- Constitution of National and State Advisory Councils.

2.5 NORMS AND STANDARDS FOR A SCHOOL

Sl. No.	*Item*	*Norms and Standards*	
1. Number of teachers:			
(a)	For Ist to 5th class	Admitted children	No. of teachers
		Up to 60	2
		61-90	3
		91-120	4
		121-200	5
		Above 150 children	5 plus 1 Head-teacher
		Above 200	Pupil-Teacher Ratio (excluding Head-teacher) shall not exceed forty.
(b)	For 6th to 8th class	(1) At least one teacher pre-class so that there shall be at least one teacher each for— (i) Science and Mathematics; (ii) Social Studies; (iii) Languages. (2) At least one teacher for every thirty-five children. (3) Where admission of children is above one hundred—	

(*Contd.*)

Sl. No.	*Item*	*Norms and Standards*
		(i) A full time head-teacher; (ii) Part time instructors for— (A) Art Education; (B) Health and Physical Education; (C) Work Education.
2. Building		All-weather building consisting of— (i) At least one class-room for every teacher and an office-cum-store-cum-Head teacher's room; (ii) Barrier-free access; (iii) Separate toilets for boys and girls; (iv) Safe and adequate drinking water facility to all children; (v) A kitchen where mid-day meal is cooked in the school; (vi) Playground;
General Observations:		1. Observations on Norms and standards of a school are taken of separately. 2. Science and mathematics should not be clubbed together. 3. No provision is made for co-scholastic or co-curricular activities. 4. Prescribed pupil-teacher ration is quite high.

In most of the public schools in Delhi overall pupil teacher ratio is 20 : 1. It is very clear that for maintaining standards in education pupil-teacher ratio must be less than 20. From the norms as given in Right to Education it is obvious that state schools which usually try to conform to norms will not be able to provide quality education.

The salient features of this Bill are:

- Children between 6 and 14 years are to be provided free and compulsory education.
- Schools must not fail kids up to Class VIII.
- Schools must admit children without school leaving certificates.
- Penalties for taking fees.
- Penalties for subjecting children or parents to screening procedures.
- Penalties for curriculum not being consistent with the Constitution of India.
- Penalties for ignoring social responsibility.
- Private schools to provide 25 percent seats to weaker sections.
- Teachers who are not adequately qualified have 5 years to acquire necessary qualifications.
- Inclusion of children who are disadvantaged because of disability.

3

Directive Principles and Education in India

Articles 36 to 51 of the Constitution deal with the Directive Principles of State Policy.

At the commencement of the Constitution Article 45 provided that the State shall strive to provide within ten years from the commencement of the Constitution free and compulsory education to all children up to 14 years of age. The State's liability has since been amended to cover children between 6-14 years of age.

Enrolment figures for Elementary Education in India (2003) reveal that in the year 2003-2004 there were 1,224 lakh children (classes 1-VIII) enrolled of which 468 lakhs were in the age group 11-14. The target set at the commencement of the Constitution is however yet to be achieved.

The parliament has passed the Constitution Amendment Act, 2002 to make elementary education a Fundamental Right. for children in the age group of 6-14years.

In 2001 the Central government launched the scheme of *Sarva Shiksha Abhiyan*. The goals of the Abhiyan are as follows:

(i) All 6-14 age children in School/Education Guarantee Scheme Center/ bridge course by 2003,

(ii) All 6-14 age children complete five year primary education by 2007

(iii) All 6-14 age children complete eight years of schooling by 2010

(iv) Focus on elementary education of satisfactory quality with emphasis on education for life

(v) Bridge all gender and social category gaps at primary stage by 2007 and at elementary education level by 2010 and

(vi) Universal retention by 2010.

The Central and the State governments share 50-50 expenditure on the Sarva Shiksha Abhiyan The programme covers the entire country with special focus on educational needs of girls, SCs/STs and other children in difficult circumstances. The Abhiyan plans to open new schools in areas where such facilities do not already exist and also to strengthen existing school infra structure by providing extra class rooms, toilets, drinking water facilities and school improvement grants. A number of initiatives like free supply of text books target children from economically and socially backward sections of the community. The digital divide is proposed to be covered by providing computers even in schools in rural areas.

By December 2004, the Central government had released Rs. 4,386.47 crore to the States and the Union Territories.

During the year 2004-2005 2,108 school buildings and 82,538 additional class rooms had been constructed. Toilet facilities had been provided in over fifty thousand schools while drinking water facilities had been provided in 44, 322 schools all over the country. Over two lakh new teachers had been appointed. Free text books had been provided to 6.15 crore children.

An important component of the Sarva Shiksha Abhiyan are the *Education Guarantee Scheme (EGS)* and *Alternative and Innovative Education (AIE)*. These components are intended to bring out of school children in the fold of Elementary Education. EGS addresses areas where schools do not exist within 1 km and at least 15-25 children of 6-14 age group are out of school. In hill regions even 10 students are enough for being covered under the EGS. AEI is for special category of children like migrating children street children and child labour.

Bridge courses have been designed for the benefit of children who dropped out before completing their elementary education. Bridge courses and back to school camps can be residential or non-residential depending on the need of the children.

District Primary Education Programme (DPEP). A major initiative to revitalize the primary education system and achieve the objective of universalization was launched by the Centre in 1994. The key strategies of the scheme are to retain the contextuality and sensitivity to local conditions and ensuring full participation of the community. DPEP is based on the principle of additionality. It is structured to fill the existing gaps by providing inputs over and above the provisions made under Central and State sector schemes for primary education.

The programme components include construction of class rooms, opening of Non-formal/Alternative Schooling Centers, appointment of new teachers, setting up early childhood education centers and setting up of Block Resource Centers.

DPEP has so far opened more than 1,60,000 new schools. The Alternative School centers cover nearly 3.5 million children while another 2c lakh children are covered by bridge courses of different types. In the districts covered by DPEP and other schemes, the enrolment was above 85 per cent.

Operation Black Board (OBB) launched in 1987-88 has since been merged with the Sarva Shiksha Abhiyan since 2002-2003. OBB had aimed at providing at least two reasonably large rooms, at least two teachers and essential teaching material for every existing primary school. OBB however could not cover the entire spectrum of schools.

In Rajasthan two projects for universalisation of primary education need special mention. *Lok Jumbish* Project was launched to achieve education for all through people's mobilization. The project has since been integrated in *Sarva Shiksha Abhiyan*.

Shiksha Karmi **Project** gave primacy to education of girls. The project provides primary education in day schools and schools of convenient timings. The project identifies teacher absenteeism as the main obstacle in achieving the goal of universalization of primary education.

4

Constitution and Educational Development

Education subject to some provisions relating to higher education was placed in the State List when the Constitution was framed. Constitution was amended in 1976 and education was placed in the Concurrent List.

4.1 EDUCATION IN THE CONCURRENT LIST

The Forty-Second Constitutional Amendment, 1976, affected the role of Central and State Governments in education.

Education in the Concurrent List implies that the Central Government as well as State Governments are responsible for the promotion of education. Entry 25 of the Concurrent List states, "Education includes technical education, medical education and university education subject to the provisions of entries 63, 64, 65 and 66 of List I, vocational and technical training of labour".

Entries 63, 64, 65 and 66 of List I (Central List) pertain to Central Universities, Institutions of National Importance, coordination and determination of standards in institutions for higher education research and scientific and technical institutions.

In case of any dispute between the Central Government and the State Government, legislation framed by the Central Government will have overriding authority.

4.2 VARIOUS CONSTITUTIONAL PROVISIONS RELATING TO EDUCATION

1. *Article 21A. Right to Education*: The State shall provide free and compulsory education to all children of the age of six to fourteen years in such a manner as the State may, by law determine. [Inserted by the Constitution (Eighty-sixth Amendment) Act, 2002].

2. *Article 27. Freedom as to Payment of Taxes for Promotion of any Particular Religion*: No person shall be compelled to pay any taxes, the proceeds of which are specifically appropriated in payment of expenses for the promotion or maintenance of any particular religion or religious denomination.

3. *Article 28. Freedom as to Attendance at Religious Instruction or Religious Worship in Certain Educational Institutions*:

(i) No religious instruction shall be provided in any educational institution wholly maintained out of State funds.

(ii) Nothing in Clause (i) shall apply to an educational institution which is administered by the State but has been established under any endowment or trust which requires that religious instruction shall be imparted in such institution.

(iii) No person attending any educational institution, recognised by the State or receiving aid out of State funds, shall be required to take part in any religious instruction that may be imparted in such institution or to attend any religious worship that may be conducted in such institution or in any premises attached thereto unless such person or, if such person is a minor, his guardian has given his consent.

4. *Article 29. Protection of Interests of Minorities*: (1) Any section of the citizens residing in the territory of India or any part thereof having a distinct language, script or culture of its own shall have the right to conserve the same.

(2) No citizen shall be denied admission into any educational institution maintained by the State or receiving aid out of State funds on grounds only of religion, race, caste, language or any of them.

5. *Article 30. Right of Minorities to Establish and Administer Educational Institutions*: (1) All minorities, whether based on religion or language, shall have the right to establish and administer educational institutions of their choice.

(2) In making any law providing for the compulsory acquisition of any property of an educational institution established and administered by a minority, referred to in clause (1), the State shall ensure that the amount fixed or determined under such law for the acquisition of such property is such as would not restrict or abrogate the right guaranteed under the clause.

(3) The State shall not, in granting aid to educational institutions, discriminate against any educational institution on the ground that it is under the management of a minority, whether based on religion or language.

6. *Article 45. Provision for Early Childhood Care and Education to Children Below the Age of Six Years*: The State shall endeavour to provide early childhood care and education for all children until they complete the age of six years. (Substituted for the original Article 45 by the Constitution Eighty-Sixth Amendment Act, 2002.)

7. *Article 96. Promotion of Educational and Economic Interests of Scheduled Castes, Scheduled Tribes and Other Weaker Sections*: The State shall promote with special care the educational and economic interests of the weaker sections of the people, and in particular, of the Scheduled Castes

and the Scheduled Tribes and shall protect them from social injustice and all forms of exploitation.

8. *Article 51A. Fundamental Duties*: It shall be the duty of every citizen of India who is a parent or guardian to provide opportunities for education to his child or ward as the case may be, between the age of six and fourteen years. [Inserted by the Constitution (Eighty-sixth Amendment) Act, 2002.]

9. *Article 337. Special Provision with Respect to Educational Grants for the Benefit of Anglo-Indian Community*: During the first three financial years after the commencement of this Constitution, the same grants, if any, shall be made by the Union and by each State for the benefit of the Anglo-Indian community in respect of education as were made in the financial year ending on the thirty-first day of March, 1948.

During every succeeding period of three years the grants may be less by ten per cent, than those for the immediately preceding period of three years:

Provided that at the end of ten years from the commencement of this Constitution such grants, to the extent to which they are a special concession to the Anglo-Indian community shall cease:

Provided further that no educational institution shall be entitled to receive any grant under this article unless at least forty per cent of the annual admissions therein are made available to members of communities other than the Anglo-Indian community.

10. *Article 350. Language to be Used in Representations for Redress of Grievances*: Every person shall be entitled to submit a representation for the redress of any grievance to any officer or authority of the Union or a State in any of the languages used in the Union or in the State, as the case may be.

11. *Article 350A. Facilities for Instruction in Mother-Tongue at Primary Stage*: It shall be the endeavour of every State and of every local authority within the State to provide adequate facilities for instruction in the mother-tongue at the primary stage of education to children belonging to linguistic minority groups and the President may issue such directions to any State as he considers necessary or proper for securing the provision of such facilities.

12. *Article 350B. Special Officer for Linguistic Minorities*: (i) There shall be a Special Officer for linguistic minorities to be appointed by the President.

(ii) It shall be the duty of the Special Officer to investigate all matters relating to the safeguards provided for linguistic minorities under this Constitution and report to the President upon those matters at such intervals as the President may direct, and the President shall cause all such reports to be laid before each House of Parliament, and sent to the Government of the States concerned.

13. *Article 351. Directive for Development of the Hindi Language*: It shall be the duty of the Union to promote the spread of the Hindi language, to develop it so that it may serve as a medium of expression for all the elements of the composite culture of India and to secure its enrichment by assimilating without interfering with its genius, the forms, style and expressions used in Hindustani and in the other languages of India specified in the Eighth Schedule, and by drawing, wherever necessary or desirable for its vocabulary, primarily of Sanskrit and secondarily other languages.

14. *Higher Education and Research*: Parliament has the exclusive rights to enact legislation in respect of institutions and Union Agencies mentioned in entries 62, 63, 64, 65 and 66 of list-I (Union List).

Union agencies and institutions for—

(a) professional, vocational or technical training including the training of police officers; or

(b) the promotion of special studies of research; or

(c) scientific or technical assistance in the investigation or detection of crime.

(62) The institutions known at the commencement of this Constitution as the National Library, the Indian Museum, the Imperial War Museum, the Victoria Memorial and the Indian War Memorial, and any other like institution financed by the Government of India wholly or in part and declared by the Parliament by law to be an institution of national importance.

(63) The institutions known at the commencement of this Constitution as the Banaras Hindu University, the Aligarh Muslim University and the Delhi University, and any other institution declared by Parliament by law to be an institution of national importance.

(64) Institutions for scientific or technical education financed by the Government of India wholly or in part and declared by Parliament by law to be institutions of national importance.

(65) Coordination and determination of standards in institutions for higher education or research and scientific and technical institutions.

(66) Ancient and historical monuments and records, and archaeological sites and remains, declared by or, under a law made by Parliament to be of national importance.

15. *Educational and Cultural Relations with Foreign Countries. Entry 13 of the Union List*: Participation in international conferences, associations and other bodies and implementing of decisions made these at.

4.3 EDUCATIONAL ADMINISTRATION AT THE NATIONAL LEVEL

A perusal of the constitutional provisions reveals that Central Government is expected to play a significant role in the field of education. Though

Ministry of Human Resource Development, Department of Education, Government of India (Before 1985, the Ministry was known as the Ministry of Education), discharges the major responsibility in the field of Education on behalf of the Government of India, yet there are other Ministries at the Centre which also perform functions in the field of education. Broadly speaking, following are the major functions performed by the Ministry of Human Resource Development, Government of India:

(1) *Planning*: Educational planning is a part and parcel of the total planning of the country. The Central Government determines targets and prepares the educational plan to be implemented by the country as a whole. Of course it consults State Governments.

(2) *Educational Reforms*: From time-to-time, the Government of India has set up Commissions which have gone into the various aspects of education at different levels and have provided valuable recommendations and suggestions. These recommendations have further been considered by the experts and the States requested to implement the recommendations of the expert bodies.

(3) *Organisation*: For carrying out educational plans, Government of India has set-up institutions like All-India Council of Technical Education, the National Council of Educational Research & Training, National Institute of Educational Planning and Administration which provide guidance to the States in the field of Education.

(4) *Direction*: The Central Government also directs and guides the State Governments, local bodies and private enterprise so as to encourage education on right lines. This is being done by the Ministry through the Central Advisory Board of Education.

(5) *Control*: As the State Governments require financial help from the Centre for supporting their educational programmes, they look to the Central Government for grants. The Central Government allocates suitable grants to the States, local bodies and private agencies. Thus, it exercises considerable control on education.

(6) *Equalisation of Education Opportunities*: The Government of India is wedded to the establishment of an egalitarian society and therefore has taken many steps to provide equal educational opportunities to the weaker sections of the society. It has initiated a large number of programmes in this direction.

(7) *Pilot Projects*: The Ministry of Human Resource Development, Government of India, has undertaken a large number of pilot projects like rural universities, regional institutes, curriculum reform and textbooks, etc. By starting these projects, the Ministry aims at providing enlightened leadership all over the country.

(8) *Administration of Education in the Union Territory and Centrally Administered Areas*: Centre is directly responsible for education in various Union territories and other centrally administered areas.

(9) *Clearing House Function*: The Department of Education serves as a depository of information and ideas of education, research, training and statistics. From time-to-time it brings out useful information on various aspects of education. The Department of Education also published a few educational journals which have proved to be very helpful in disseminating information in the country.

10. *State Sponsored Organisations*: For carrying out educational plans, Government of India has set-up institutions like UGC, All-India Council of Technical Education, the National Council of Educational Research and Training, National Institute of Educational Planning and Administration since renamed National University of Educational Planning and Administration, which provide guidance to the States in the field of Education.

11. *Equalisation of Education Opportunities*: The Government of India is wedded to the establishment of an egalitarian society and therefore has taken many steps to provide equal educational opportunities to the weaker sections of the society. It has initiated a large number of programmes in this direction.

12. *Legislation Like Right to Education*: *Constitutional Provisions*. Earlier Article 45 related to the provision of free and compulsory elementary education. In 2002, Article 21A was inserted in the Constitution which provided for the right to free and compulsory education.

13. *Educational Schemes*: Like Sarva Shiksha Abhiyan (SSA), Vocationalisation of Education, Mid-day Meals, Improvement of Science Education, Computer Literacy, Revamping of Teacher Education etc. are being undertaken and necessary help provided to States for their implementation.

14. *Protection of Minorities Rights*. Several steps have been taken to protect the right of minorities to manage educational institutes as provided under Article 30.

15. *Promotion of Educational and Economic Interests of Scheduled Castes, Scheduled Tribes and Other Weaker Sections*. Article 46 relates to this aspect.

16. *Facilities for Instruction in Mother Tongue*. Article 350A assures this.

17. *High Education and Research*. The State takes several measures for the promotion of Higher Education through University Grants Commission, National Council of Teacher Education and All India Council for Technical Education.

18. *Central Advisory Board of Education* (*CABE*). This is the highest

advisory body constituted by the State to advise the Central and State Governments on policy matters.

19. *Educational Relations with Foreign Countries.* The State send delegates to other countries to attend educational conferences etc. and implements decisions taken.

20. *Guidelines for Determining Aims and Objectives of Education.* The State lays down guidelines of educational policies relating to aims and objectives of education. Dr. Radhakrishnan had very rightly observed, "Our educational system must find the guiding principles in the aims of social order for which it prepares".

4.4 MAJOR AUTONOMOUS ORGANISATIONS AND INSTITUTIONS UNDER MINISTRY OF HUMAN RESOURCE DEVELOPMENT FOR IMPLEMENTING CONSTITUTIONAL PROVISIONS

1. Central Advisory Board of Education (CABE)
2. National Council of Educational Research and Training (NCERT)
3. National Council for Teacher Education (NITE)
4. National University of Educational Planning and Administration (NUEPA)
5. University Grants Commission (UGC)
6. All India Council for Technical Education (AICTE)
7. Central Board of Secondary Education (CBSE)
8. Kendriya Vidyalaya Sangathan (KVS)
9. Navodaya Vidyalaya Samiti (NVS)
10. National Institute of Open Schooling (NIOS)
11. Central Tibetan School Administration (CTSA)
12. National Foundation for Teacher's Welfare (NFTW)
13. Distance Education Council (DEC)
14. Indian Council for Agriculture Research (ICAR)
15. Bar Council of India (BCI)
16. Rehabilitation Council of India (RCI)
17. Medical Council of India (MCI)
18. Pharmacy Council of India (PCI)
19. Indian Nursing Council (INC)
20. Dentist Council of India (DCI)
21. Central Council of Homeopathy (CCH)
22. Central Council of Indian Medicine (CCIM)
23. Indian Council of Historical Research (ICHR)
24. Indian Council of Philosophical Research (ICPR)
25. Indian Council of Social Science Research (ICSSR)

I. CENTRAL ADVISORY BOARD OF EDUCATION (CABE)

Establishment of CABE

The Central Advisory Board of Education (CABE), the highest advisory body to advise the Central and State Governments in the field of education, was first established in 1920 and dissolved in 1923 as a measure of economy. It was revived in 1935 and had continued to be in existence till 1994. Between 1935 and 1994, it met 50 times. Practically all important matters concerning education are debated in the CABE and consensus reached. Despite the fact that in the past, important decisions had been taken on the advice of CABE and it had provided a forum for widespread consultation and examination of issues relating to educational and cultural development, it was unfortunately not reconstituted after the expiry of its extended tenure in March, 1994. It was revived in the year 2004. CABE has a particularly important role to play at the present juncture in view of the significant socio-economic and socio-cultural developments taking place in the country and for the review of the national Policy on Education which is also due. It is a matter of importance, therefore, that the Central and State Governments, and educationists and people representing all interests, should increase their interaction and evolve a participative process of decision making in education, which enhances the federal structure of our polity.

Functions of CABE

Functions of CABE are:

(a) to review the progress of education from time-to-time;

(b) to appraise the extent and manner in which the education policy has been implemented by the Central and State Governments, and other concerned agencies, and to give appropriate advice in the matter;

(c) to advise regarding coordination between the Central and State Governments/UT Administrations, State Governments and non-governmental agencies for educational development in accordance with the education policy; and

(d) to advise, *suo motu*, or on a reference made to it by the Central Government or any State Government or a Union Territory Administration on any educational question.

For the discharge of these functions, the Board may:

(i) call for information and comments from any Government institution, any other organisation or an individual;

(ii) appoint committees or groups comprising members of CABE and/or others as may be necessary; and

(iii) commission, through Government or any other agency, studies, research or reports on any specific issue requiring the attention of the Board or its committees or groups.

Composition of the Board

The composition of the Board is as under:

1. *Chairman*: Minister of Human Resource Development.
2. *Vice Chairman*: Minister of State for Human Resource Development.
3. Representatives of the Government of India including 7 Ministries and Member Education, Planning Commission.
4. Representatives of State Governments and UT Administrations – One each.
5. 4 Members of Lok Sabha, 2 Members of Rajya Sabha.
6. 15 *Ex-officio* members.
7. 31 nominated members representing different interests.
8. Member-Secretary – Secretary, Department of Secondary and Higher Education, Ministry of Human Resource Development, Government of India.

Decisions of the Union Government relating to education are enforceable only if they are taken in pursuance of central legislation, as for example, the unquestioned acceptability of the decisions taken by the statutory bodies set up by the Government of India covering various aspects of higher education. Other decisions by the Union Government have little sanctity unless they are based on consensus. The CABE provides a forum for sharing and consensus building on national issues in education among the States. The Education Commission (1964-66) refers to the CABE as the most important advisory body in the field of education. The National Policy on Education (NPE) 1986 (with modifications undertaken in 1992) states that "the CABE will play a pivotal role in reviewing educational development, determining the changes required to improve the system and monitoring implementation".

Recalling the pre-independence era, matters of far-reaching importance considered by the CABE pertain to various educational issues. In 1938, the CABE set up a Committee on the Wardha Education Scheme (*Nai Taleem* of Mahatma Gandhi). The Committee went into great detail in working out modalities for the implementation of the *Nai Taleem* and recommended it for adoption by all provincial governments at that time. This was reiterated by the CABE Committee on "Post-War Plan for Educational Development in India" (1944), also known as Sargent Plan. This was a Plan for Indianisation of education, to universalise primary education, and to improve quality of education so that our education system became comparable with that of the industrialised nations.

The CABE secured a national consensus on the structure of education, namely the '10+2+3 pattern', made recommendation towards establishment of 'Common School System' as the bedrock of educational quality, social cohesion and national integration calling for moving towards a common admission policy, tuition-free school, etc.

After 2004, the National Curriculum Framework (2005) was approved by CABE.

The CABE has set up a number of Committees to review various dimensions of education.

II. NATIONAL COUNCIL OF EDUCATIONAL RESEARCH AND TRAINING (NCERT)

An Apex Organisation in School Education

The NCERT was set up by the Government of India in 1961 as an autonomous organisation registered under Societies Registration Act (Act XXI of 1880) to advise and assist the Ministry of Human Resource Development, Government of India and Department of Education in States/Union Territories in formulation and implementation of their policies and major programmes in the field of education, particularly for qualitative improvement of social education.

Organisational Structure

The Union Minister of Human Resource Development is the President (*ex-officio*) of the General Body of the NCERT. The members of the General Body include the Education Ministers of all States and Union Territories. Other members of the General Body include the Chairperson of the University Grants Commission (UGC): the Secretary to the Government of India. Ministry of Human Resource Development (Department of Education); four Vice-Chancellors of Universities (one from each region); the Chairman of the Central Board of Secondary Education; the Commissioner of the Kendriya Vidyalaya Sangathan; the Director, Central Health Education Bureau; the Director of Training, Directorate General of Training and Employment, Ministry of Labour; one representative of the Education Division, Planning Commission; all the members of the Executive Committee (not included above) of the Council and such other persons, not exceeding six, nominated by the Government of India (not less than four of them shall be school teachers). The Secretary, NCERT is the Convener of the General Body of the NCERT.

Functions

For the realisation of the above objectives, NCERT undertakes the following programmes and activities:

1. *Research*: Conducts, aids promotes and coordinates research in all branches of school education.

2. *Teacher Education*: Organisation pre-service and in-service training of teachers mainly at an advanced level.

3. *Extension Services*: Organises extension services for institutions, organisations and agencies engaged in educational reconstruction.

4. *Experiments and Innovations*: Develops and experiments with improved educational techniques, practices and innovations.

5. *Clearing House of Data and Information*: Collects, compiles and disseminates educational information.

6. *Assistance to States*: Assists the States and the State-level institutions, organisations and agencies in developing and implementing programmes for qualitative improvement of school education.

7. *International Collaboration*: Collaborates with international organisations like UNESCO, UNICEF, etc. and with national-level educational institutions of other countries.

8. *Publications*: Undertakes the preparations and/or the publications of books, materials, periodicals and other literature.

9. *Nodal Agency*: Serves as the nodal agency of universalisation of elementary education.

The National Council of Educational and Research runs the following:

1. National Institute of Education (NIE), New Delhi.
2. Central Institute of Educational Technology (CIET), New Delhi.
3. Pt. Sundarlal Sharma Central Institute of Vocational Education (PSSCIVE), Bhopal.
4. Five Regional Institutes of Education (RIEs) – Ajmer, Bhopal, Bhubaneswar, Mysore and Shillong.

Departments of the National Institute of Education (NIE)

1. Department of Elementary Education.
2. Department of Education of Groups with special needs.
3. Department of Women's Studies.
4. Department of Education in Science and Mathematics.
5. Department of Teacher Education and Extension.
6. Department of Education in Social Sciences and Humanities.
7. Department of Educational Psychology and Foundations of Education.
8. Department of Educational Measurement and Evaluation.
9. Department of Educational Surveys and Data Processing.
10. Department of Educational Research and Policy Perspective.
11. Department of Computer Education and Technological Aids.
12. Publication Department.
13. Planning, Programming, Monitoring and Evaluation Division.
14. International Relations Division.
15. Division of Library, Documentation and Information.

III. NATIONAL COUNCIL FOR TEACHER EDUCATION (NCTE)

The NCTE, set up in 1973 was given a statutory recognition by a gazette notification issued on August 17, 1995 (Notification No. 484) by the Ministry of Human Resource Development (Department of Education). This was done in pursuance of the National Council for Teacher Education Act, 1993 (No. 73 of 1993). This Act has been enacted with a view to achieving planned and coordinated development of the Teacher Education system throughout the country, the regulation and proper maintenance of norms and standards in the teacher education system and for matters connected therewith. According to the Act "Teacher Education" includes programmes of education, research or training of persons for equipping them to teach at pre-primary, primary, secondary and senior secondary stages in schools, and includes non-formal education, part-time education, adult education and correspondence education. It is further provided in the Act that every institution offering or intending to offer a course or training in Teacher Education on or after 17th August 1995 is to seek recognition in accordance with this Act by making an application to the respective Regional Committee of the NCTE. Further, any institution which has been recognised under the Act has to seek permission to start any new course or training in Teacher Education by making an application to the Regional Committee of the NCTE.

Programmes/Functions

1. *Recognition of Institutions*: The NCTE attempts to recognise institutions and courses only after ensuring that teacher training institutions have adequate building space, qualified teacher educators and availability of other infrastructure in the institutions. Its guidelines also stipulate that all of them offer full-time academic programmes leading to BEd or other degrees. Another important condition is regarding the pupil-teacher ratio which has been fixed at 1:10.

2. *Check on Correspondence Courses in Teacher Education*: In view of the proliferation of sub-standard teacher training institutions in the country offering BEd programmes through correspondence courses—some of them admitting as 30,000 students a year purely for commercial considerations—the NCTE stipulated stringent conditions for running such courses in future.

The NCTE has laid down clearly that correspondence programme leading to BEd degree can be offered only to clear the backlog of untrained teachers for the present and that not more than 500 students can be enrolled by an institution in a year.

The other conditions laid down include that teachers seeking admission should have put in three-year service in a recognised school and that the duration of the programme will be for two years, with contact programme during two consecutive summer vacations—the intervening period taking care of correspondence lessons.

3. *Prohibition of Changing Capitation Fee*: The NCTE has also categorically disapproved charging capitation fee from students. Commercialisation has been defined as the total receipts (including those from students per year) exceeding recurring expenditure of the programme by more than 10 per cent.

4. *In-Service Education*: In order to help teachers already working in the system to keep abreast of the latest in education, the NCTE has proposed that they should compulsorily undergo in-service teacher training programmes at least once in five years and accumulate credits. Such programmes are to be conducted by the existing institutions including DIETs and university departments of education.

5. *Curriculum Framework for Teacher Education*: In 1996, NCTE prepared and circulated a curriculum framework for teacher education at various levels. The framework outlined concerns that teacher education should take note of, objectives of teacher education and several related issues.

6. *Norms and Standards*: NCTE has set up norms and standards for establishing different types of courses right from E.C.C.E./Pre-primary to M.Ed.

Regional Committees

Four regional committees of the Council have been set up at Jaipur, Bangalore, Bhubaneswar and Bhopal, for Northern, Southern, Eastern and Western regions respectively. These Regional Committees primarily look after and recognition of teacher training institutions in their regions and are empowered to grant permission to institutions to run teacher training courses as per provisions of the National Council for Teacher Education Act.

Number of Recognised Teacher Education Institutions. As on 31 January 2006, about 6000 teacher training institutions exist offering about 6600 courses with an intake of 5.50 lakh teacher trainee.

IV. NATIONAL UNIVERSITY OF EDUCATIONAL PLANNING AND ADMINISTRATION (NUEPA) (FORMERLY KNOWN AS NATIONAL INSTITUTE OF EDUCATIONAL PLANNING AND ADMINISTRATION – NIEPA)

Brief History of NUEPA

NUEPA has its origin dating back to 1962 when the UNESCO established the Asian Regional Centre for Educational Planners and Administrators which later became the Asian Institute of Educational Planning and

Administration in 1965. After 4 years of its existence, it was taken over by the Government of India and renamed as the National Staff College for Educational Planners and Administrators. Subsequently, with the increased roles and functions of the National Staff College, particularly in capacity building, research and professional support services to governments, it was again renamed as the National Institute of Educational Planning and Administration (NIEPA) in 1979.

NIEPA was conferred the status of Deemed to be University in August 2006 and its nomenclature was changed to NUEPA.

Objectives

- Organising pre-service and in-service training programmes in the area of educational planning and administration and allied disciplines;
- Undertaking, aiding, promoting and coordinating research in various aspects of educational planning and administration and allied disciplines, including comparative studies in planning techniques and administrative procedures in the different States of India and in other countries of the world;
- Providing academic and professional guidance to agencies and institutions engaged in educational planning and administration;
- Offering M. Phil, Ph. D. and Post-Doctoral Programmes and awards degrees in educational planning, educational administration, educational finance, comparative education, school education, higher education, professional education, discrimination in education, educational management and information system, etc.;
- Acting as a clearing house of ideas and information on research, training and extension in educational planning and administration services and other programmes;
- Preparing, printing and publishing papers, periodicals and books in furtherance of these objectives and especially to bring out a Journal on Educational Planning and Administration;
- Organising training, conferences, workshops, meetings, seminars and briefing sessions for educational personnel of the Central and State Governments and Union Territories;
- Offering, on request, consultancy service to Governments, including State Governments, educational institutions and institutions/organisations in India and abroad.
- Organising orientation and training programmes and refresher courses for teacher-educators and for University and College Administrators engaged in educational planning and administration;

- Awarding consultancy work/services to other organisations/ individuals;
- Collaborating with other agencies, institutions and organisations, including the University Grants Commission, the Universities, Institutes of Management and Administration and other allied institutions in India and abroad, in such way as may be considered necessary for the promotion of these objectives;
- Providing, on request, facilities for training and research in educational planning and administration to other countries, especially of the Asian Region, and collaborate with them in programmes;
- Offering fellowships, scholarships and academic awards in furtherance of the objects of the National University;
- Conferring honorary fellowships on eminent educationists for their contribution in the field of educational planning and administration;
- Undertaking extra mural studies, extension programme and field outreach activities to contribute to the development of society;
- Disseminating and advancing knowledge by providing instructional, research and extension facilities in such branches of learning as it may deem fit and providing to students and teachers the necessary facilities and atmosphere for the promotion of innovations in education leading to restructuring of courses, new methods of teaching and learning, and integral development of personality, studies in various disciplines, inter-disciplinary studies, and National integration & International understanding;
- Conducting the above-mentioned programmes and courses in its off-Campuses and off-shore campuses; and
- Doing or performing all such other acts, functions and things as may be deemed desirable or incidental by the National University in furtherance of the above objectives of the National University.

Departments of NUEPA

The National University comprises of ten Departments, which are:

(i) Department of Educational Planning;
(ii) Department of Educational Administration;
(iii) Department of Educational Policy;
(iv) Department of Educational Finance;
(v) Department of School and Non-formal Education;
(vi) Department of Higher and Professional Education;
(vii) Department of Comparative Education and International Cooperation;

(viii) Department of Sub-national Systems; and
(ix) Department of Educational Management Information Systems.

V. ALL INDIA COUNCIL FOR TECHNICAL EDUCATION (AICTE)

An Apex Advisory Body on Technical Education: Functions

The All India Council for Technical Education (AICTE) was established in 1945 by the Government of India. The organisation was set up as an Apex Advisory Body to conduct survey on facilities on technical education and to promote and develop technical education in the country. National policy of Education (1986) defines AICTE as the statutory authority for planning, formulation and maintenance of norms and standards, quality assurance through accreditation, funding in priority areas, monitoring and evaluation, maintaining parity of certification and awards and ensuring coordinated and integrated development and management of technical education in the country.

The Purview of All India Council for Technical Education

AICTE covers programmes of technical education including training and research in Engineering, Technology, Architecture, Town Planning, Management, Pharmacy, Applied Arts and Crafts, Hotel Management and Catering Technology etc. at different levels.

Structure of AICTE

In accordance with the provisions of AICTE Act (1987) for the first five years after its inception in 1988, the Minister of Human Resource Development — Government of India was the Chairman of the Council. However, the first full time chairman was appointed in July 1993. The AICTE has its Headquarters in New Delhi which has the offices of the Chairman, Vice-Chairman and the Member Secretary and is presently housed in a building located in Indira Gandhi Sports Complex, Indraprastha Estate, New Delhi.

National Accreditation Board

AICTE strives to maintain the quality of technical education in the country. The National Board of Accreditation — NBA of AICTE aims to maintain level of some of the programme offered in technical Institutions on par with the programmes offered in Institutions across USA and Europe, by inducing a quality auditing system and establishing a datum for measuring the quality and excellence in engineering education.

The Bureaus of AICTE

The AICTE comprises of nine Bureaus, namely:

- Faculty Development (FD) Bureau
- Undergraduate Education (UG) Bureau
- Postgraduate Education and Research (PGER) Bureau
- Quality Assurance (QA) Bureau
- Planning and Coordination (PC) Bureau
- Research and Institutional Development (RID) Bureau
- Administration (Admin) Bureau
- Finance (Fin) Bureau
- Academic (Acad.) Bureau

VI. UNIVERSITY GRANTS COMMISSION (UGC)

The UGC is a statutory organisation established by an Act of Parliament in 1956 for the promotion, development and coordination of college and university education. It has the power to fix standards in teaching, examination and research in the college and university education system. The Act has been amended from time to time as situations have demanded.

Functions of UGC

The important functions of the UGC are:

1. To promote and coordinate university and college education.
2. To inquire into the financial needs of universities and colleges.
3. To allocate and disburse grants to universities established or incorporated by or under a Central Act for the maintenance and development of such a university or for any other general or specific purpose.
4. To recommend to any university the measures necessary for the improvement of university education.
5. To advise the Central and State Governments to allocate grants to universities for any general or specific purpose out of the Consolidated Fund of India or the State, as the case may be.
6. To advise any authority, if required, on the establishment of a new university or the expansion of activities of any university.
7. To advise the Central or any State Government or University or any question which may be referred to the Commission by the Central or the State Government or the University as the case may be.
8. To collect information on all such matters relating to university education in India and abroad.

9. To require a university to furnish it with such information as case may be needed relating to the financial position of the university or the studies in the various branches of learning undertaken in that university.

10. To perform such other functions as may be deemed necessary by the Commission for advancing the causes of higher education.

Regional Offices

The UGC was decentralised its working by opening seven regional offices at Bhopal, Kolkata, Guwahati, Delhi, Hyderabad, Bangalore and Pune.

4.5 THE ROLE OF STATE IN EDUCATION

Broadly speaking there are three schools of thought concerning the relationship that should exist between State and education.

One school of thought favours the total socialisation of education. According to its protagonists the state should have a full and unfettered say in the domain of education, it should dictate the content, the aim and even the method of education. There is no scope for private enterprise in education. This point may be fully illustrated by the Nazi and Fascist schools and even the Communist schools in Russia.

Two, according to the theory of *laissez faire* education should be the concern of the family, the church or philanthropy. The State interference means jeopardising the rights of the parents, priests and children. If State interferes, formally in the formulation of educational policies and their administration, the considerations of party in power and its interests are likely to have an adverse effect of the functioning of educational policies.

In ancient India, the State took several steps to promote education. It, however, did not interfere in the functioning of the educational institutions. It made liberal grants to the institutes of higher learning and patronised men of letters. The standard of education imparted in institutions of higher education, namely Nalanda, Taxila (Takshila), Vikramshila etc. was so high that students and scholars flocked to India. Indian scholars were in high demand in countries like Tibet and China etc.

Three, there is another view that has assumed importance in recent times and which strikes a balance between these two extreme views. This view envisages full cooperation between the State, the family and the church in the matter of educating the child and the drawing out the best that is within him. According to this view, the State should neither keep its hands off education nor should it lay its hands on every educational matter. This policy is being followed in India.

4.6 STATE MANAGEMENT AND STATE CONTROL OF EDUCATION

State management of education implies that the educational institutions in the State are brought into existence by the State, are financed by it through the government offices and are also administered by persons directly appointed by the government. There are no educational institutions other than the government.

State control of education means the overall control exercised by the State over educational institutions. There are educational institutions financed and managed by bodies other than the government. These bodies may be educational trusts, religious bodies, local boards, social bodies, etc.

State management of educational institutions is likely to bring red tapism and smother all initiatives and inventiveness. The private institutions have greater chances of going in for educational experimentation for the heads of these institutions and their masters are always ready to decide upon things in a quicker and better way.

Educational Enterprises

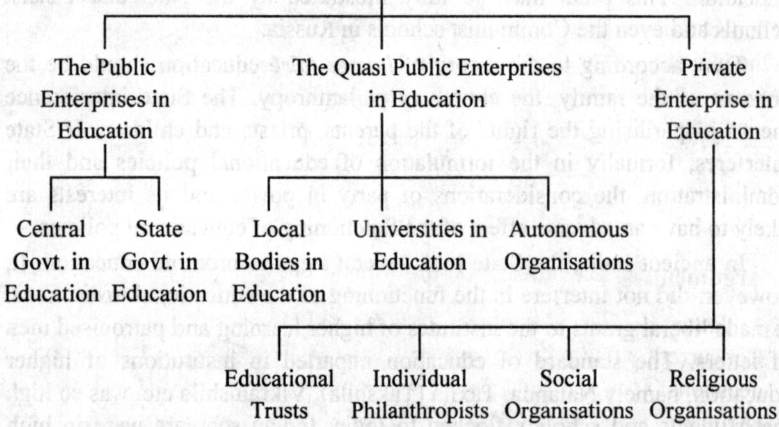

4.7 NEED FOR AN EFFECTIVE AND HEALTHY STATE CONTROL: ROLE OF THE INDIAN STATE

In the democratic structure when the government is through and through responsible for the education of its people, when it has decided to prepare the children for the social order which it wants to build up, it is but inevitable that the State should adequately supervise, guide and control the educational system. It adopts the following methods for the purpose of effective control over education:

1. *Laying Down Educational Policies*: It lays down the educational policy relating to the aims and objectives which all educational institutions in the country are expected to follow.

2. *Appointment of Educational Committees and Commissions*: It appoints committees and commissions for studying the prevailing conditions in the different stages of the educational ladder and suggesting suitable steps for the eradication of defects. It makes these recommendations available to the educational institutions for the necessary reforms which are to be undertaken.

3. *State Run Educational Institutions*: It starts and manages different type of educational institutions at various levels – Navodaya Vidyalayas, Central Schools, IITs and IIMs, etc.

4. *Guidelines on Contents*: It suggests broad guidelines on curricula, various courses of study, etc.

5. *Research and Experimentation*: It makes suitable arrangements for research and experimentation in the field of education and finances institutions of higher education and research, training and experimentation.

6. *Grants to Educational Institutions*: It gives sufficient sums as grant-in-aid to the institutions other than those of the government.

7. *Appointment of Supervision etc.*: It appoints officers whose function is to inspect and supervise the work of the various institutions and to see that certain minimum standards of instructional efficiency, discipline and the like are maintained.

8. *Planning*: Educational planning is a part and parcel of the total planning of the country.

4.8 CONTROVERSY ON PUTTING EDUCATION IN THE CONCURRENT LIST

Arguments in Favour of Making Education as a Concurrent Subject

1. *Better Implementation of Education Policies*: With education as a Concurrent subject, the States will become more serious in implementing decisions. It is said that we failed to achieve the Constitutional directive (Article 45) because the State Governments did not come up to the expectations. When education is on the Concurrent list, the Centre will ensure that the States implement its decisions in right earnest.

2. *Better Utilisation of Funds*: It has been noticed that States get money from the Centre for the purpose of education but spend them elsewhere. When the funds are allocated by the Central Government, it is in the fitness of things that it should have a say in their utilisation.

3. *Quality Leadership from the Central Government*: We are having leadership crisis in the field of education. The result is lack of direction. The Centre should provide effective leadership. This should not be taken as a

reflection on the intelligentia in the States but Centre is better equipped to provide education leadership at the national level.

4. *Improvement in Standards*: Education being a Concurrent subject, all India level of research in the field of education will improve and the research findings will be better utilised at the national and state levels.

5. *Ensuring a Uniform Structure of Education*: It is easier to follow a uniform structure in the entire country.

Arguments against Making Education a Concurrent Subject

There are also educationists who advocate that education should remain a State subject. They advance the following arguments:

1. *Based on Democratic Values*. Democracy believes in decentralisation of powers. Why should then education be a Concurrent subject, they ask?

2. *States have Better Appreciation of Local Needs*: The State Government knows the needs of its inhabitants better. The Centre cannot appreciate the educational needs of a remote village school say in Rajasthan or Tamil Nadu. So let education remain in the hands of the States.

3. *Free from Red Tape*. The bureaucrats at the Centre interfere with it. The implementation of decisions is delayed. States need to seek clearance from the Centre. If we want education to remain free from bureaucracy, it should be a state subject.

4. *Unity in Diversity*. There is 'Unity in Diversity' in India. In such a scenario, each State may have its own pattern of education to preserve the element of 'Unity in Diversity'.

National Policy on Education (1986 and as amended in 1992): Meaningful Partnership

The policy has supported the element of concurrency in education. Concurrency implies a meaningful partnership between the Central Government and State Governments. The policy states, "The Constitutional Amendment of 1976, which includes Education in the Concurrent List, was a far-reaching step whose implications – substantive, financial and administrative require a new sharing of responsibility between the Union Government and the States in respect of this vital area of national life. While the role and responsibility of the States in regard to education will remain essentially unchanged, the Union Government will accept a larger responsibility. The NPE envisages the following functions of the Union Government:

(i) to reinforce the national and integrative character of education, (ii) to maintain quality and standards (including those of the teaching profession at all levels), (iii) to study and monitor the educational requirements of the country as a whole in regard to manpower for development, (iv) to cater to the needs of research and advanced study, (v) to look after the international aspects of education, culture and human resource development and, (vi) to promote excellence at all levels of the educational pyramid throughout the country.

The policy further states, "concurrency signifies a partnership which is at once meaningful and challenging, the National Policy will be reoriented towards giving effect to it in letter and spirit".

5

Educational Schemes for the Implementation of Constitutional Provisions

Before 1976, as stated earlier, education was the exclusive responsibility of the States. The Constitutional Amendment of 1976, which included education in the Concurrent List, was a far-reaching step. The financial and administrative implications required a new sharing of responsibility between the Union Government and the States. While the role and responsibility of the States in education remained largely unchanged, the Union Government accepted a larger responsibility of reinforcing the national and integrated character of education, maintaining quality and standards including those of the teaching profession at all levels, and the study and monitoring of the educational requirements of the country.

The Central Government plays a leading role in the evolution and monitoring of the educational policies and programmes, the most notable of which are the National Policy on Education (NPE), 1986 and the Programme of Action (POA), 1986 as updated in 1922. The modified policy envisages a National System of education to bring about uniformity in education, making adult education programmes a mass movement providing universal access, retention and quality in elementary education, special emphasis, on education of girls, establishment of pace-setting schools like Navodaya Vidyalayas in each district, vocationalisation of secondary education, synthesis of knowledge and inter disciplinary research in higher education, starting more Open Universities in the States, strengthening of the All India Council of Technical Education, encouraging sports, physical education, Yoga and adoption of an effective evaluation method, etc. Besides, a decentralised management structure had also been suggested to ensure popular participation in education.

Overview: A brief review of the various schemes which have been launched by the Ministry of Human Resource Development, Government of India, for implementing the provisions on education as contained in the Constitution is attempted here.

5.1 ELEMENTARY EDUCATION

Since the formulation of the National Policy on Education—NPE (1986), and the Programme of Action—POA (1986) several new schemes for the qualitative as well as quantitative improvement of primary education and reaching the goal of UEE, have been initiated by the Government of India, Ministry of Human Resource Development (MHRD), Department of Education. Some of the old schemes have also been revised and strengthened. In this regard, a brief review of some of the major schemes are provided here:

1. Operation Blackboard (OBB)
2. District Primary Education Programme (DPEP)
3. Shiksha Karmi Project (SKP)
4. National Programme of Nutritional Support to Primary Education (NP-NSPE) or Mid-Day Meals.
5. Elementary Education as a Fundamental Right
6. Lok Jumbish (LJ)
7. Mahila Sankhya Scheme
8. Prarambhik Shiksha Kosh (ECS and AIE)
9. Sarva Shiksha Abhiyan (SSA-Education for All)
10. Education Guarantee Scheme and Alternative and Innovative Education

1. Operation Blackboard (OBB)

Objective: The scheme of Operation Blackboard started in 1987, is a Centrally Sponsored Scheme for bringing about improvement in primary education by providing additional facilities to the schools already established.

Use of the word 'Operation' indicates that there is an urgency in this programme. Its goals are clear and well-defined and the government is determined to achieve these goals with the cooperation of the people within a pre-determined time frame.

Components of the Scheme: There are three components of Operation Blackboard:

1. Provision of at least two reasonably large rooms that are usable in all weathers, with a deep veranda along with separate toilet facilities for boys and girls.
2. Provision of at least two teachers, as far as possible, one of them a woman, in every primary school.
3. Provision of essential teaching and learning materials.

Responsibility: For the operation of the Scheme, responsibility is shared by the Central Government, State Government and the local community.

Role of the community in OBB scheme is as under:

(a) Necessary land for the construction of school building including land for games and sports to be provided by the local community.
(b) The local community, preferably Village Education Committees, to give a formal undertaking that they will accept responsibility for repair and maintenance of the building.
(c) The local community also to accept responsibility for an appropriate fencing around the school compound.

Hundred per cent Central assistance is provided for appointment of an additional teacher in the single teacher schools.

2. District Primary Education Programme (DPEP)

DPEP launched in 1993 is a national initiative to achieve Universalisation of Elementary Education (UEE) through district level intervention. The overall goal of the programme is the reconstruction of primary education system to operationalise the strategy of UEE as envisaged in NPC 1986 (as updated in 1992) and its Programme of Action—POA (1992) through decentralised planning and management, disaggregated target setting, community mobilisation and population specific planning. The fundamental principle of DPEP is to evolve strategy at state and district levels. It goes beyond the conventional packages such as opening of new schools and appointing new teachers and addresses the issues of content, process, quality and equity in education.

Objectives: The objectives of DPEP are:

(i) to reduce different in enrolment, drop-out and learning achievement among gender and social groups to less than 5 per cent;
(ii) to reduce overall primary drop-out rates for all students to less than 10 per cent;
(iii) to raise average achieved levels.

Funding of DPEP: DPEP is a Centrally Sponsored Scheme and is funded by World Bank and several international organisations.

3. Shiksha Karmi Project (SKP)

Shiksha Karmi Project, started in Rajasthan in 1987, remained in operation up to June 1998. It was a scheme jointly sponsored by the Swedish International Development Agency (SIDA), the Government of India and the State of Rajasthan.

Aims of the Project:

1. Universalisation of education.
2. Checking drop-outs.
3. Qualitative improvement of primary education.

Target Area: Socio-economically backward villages in Rajasthan.

Target Group: Specially girls.

Teachers: Replacement of regular teachers by local teachers who were less qualified but specially trained. A 'Shiksha Karmi' (SK) was a local person with minimum educational qualifications of class VIII for men and class V for women. To overcome the basic lack of qualification, special training was given to these teachers.

Role of the Community: Active involvement of the Non-Government Organisations (NGOs) and the Village Education Committees (VECs).

Prehar Pathshalas (PPs): (School of Convenient Timings) providing educational programmes for out of school children who cannot attend regular day schools.

4. National Programme of Nutritional Support to Primary Education (NPNSPE) or Mid-Day Meals

The scheme was launched in 1995 with the following objectives:

(i) Improving the nutritional status of children in classes I-V in Government, Local Body and Government aided schools, and EGS and AIE Centres.

(ii) Encouraging poor children, belonging to disadvantaged sections, to attend school more regularly and help them concentrate on classroom activities.

(iii) Providing nutritional support to children of primary stage in drought affected areas during summer vacation.

5. Lok Jumbish (People's Mobilisation)

An innovative project called "Lok Jumbish"—People's movement for Education of All—with assistance from Swedish International Development Authority (SIDA) has been undertaken in Rajasthan. The basic objective of the project was to achieve education for all by the year 2000 through people's mobilisation and their participation. The LJ, has undertaken environment building activities in 5,683 villages. 383 new schools have been opened while 227 primary schools have been upgraded. An innovative and successful NFE programme launched by LJ has spread to more than 3,000 centres. The programme has close linkage with the community. The NFE centres are called "Sahaj Shiksha Centres".

6. Right to Education

The Constitution (86th Amendment) Act 2002 enacted in December 2002 seeks to make free and compulsory education a Fundamental Right for all children in the age group 6-14 years by inserting a new Article 21-A in Part III ("Fundamental Right") of the Constitution. Article 2l-A of the Constitution says that:

> *"The State shall provide free and compulsory education to all children of the age of six to fourteen years in such manner as the State may by law, determine".*

The Government is committed to facilitate the enactment of an appropriate law that would enable the realisation of making education a fundamental right as required by the constitution. Necessary action is being taken to put in place a suitable legislation envisaged under Article 21A of the Constitution.

7. Mahila Samakhya Scheme

Pursuant to the objectives of the NPE, 1986, the Mahila Samakhya Scheme was started in 1989 to translate the goals enshrined in the NPE into a concrete programme for the education and empowerment of women in rural areas particularly those from socially and economically marginalised groups. The MS scheme recognises the centrality of education in empowering women to achieve equality. The Mahila Sanghas or women's collectives at the village level provide the women a space to meet, reflect, ask questions and articulate their thoughts and needs and make informed choices.

The Mahila Sanghas though various programmes and awareness campaigns have brought about a change in the outlook of rural women and the effects can how be seen in various facets of life at home within the family, the community and at the block and panchayat levels. The programme has also focused on awareness of the need to educate the children, especially girls, to give the equal status and opportunities which has resulted in a direct impact on enrolment and retention of girls in schools.

8. Prarambhik Shiksha Kosh

A two per cent Education Cess was levied on all major Central taxes through the Finance (No.2) Act, 2004, to help finance government's commitment to quality basic education. In order to receive the proceeds of this Education Cess, the creation of a dedicated non-lapsable fund called Prarambhik Shiksha Kosh (PSK) in the Public Account was approved by Government on 6.10.2005. Formal orders constituting PSK were issued on 14.11.2005. After presentation of the Union Budget (2006-07) on 28.2.2006, PSK became a separate line item. The funds available in the PSK were utilised exclusively for Sarva Shiksha Abhiyan (SSA) and National Programme for Nutritional Support of Primary Education (MDM Scheme). The levy of education cess is a concrete step towards providing assured funding for elementary education.

The NCTE has issued new norms and standards for various teacher training programmes like CEd, DEd, BEd, DP.Ed, and MP.Ed. The new norm have been introduced to improve the quality of teacher programmes and to strengthen the infrastructural and the facilities in teacher training institutions.

9. Sarva Shiksha Abhiyan (Education for All)

Background

The Sarva Shiksha Abhiyan was taken up to fulfil the obligations of the state regarding Universal Compulsory Elementary Education (Article 45). This Article was amended in 2002 and new Article 21A was inserted. It was felt that in spite of vigorous efforts, achievement in this area was not satisfactory. A sustained effort was needed. This resulted in the launching of Sarva Shiksha Abhiyan.

The Sarva Shiksha Abhiyan was launched towards the end of the Ninth Plan in 2002 to achieve the goal of UEE through a time-bound integrated approach, in partnership with States. The programme, which aims to provide elementary education to all children in the 6-14 age group by 2010, is an effort to improve the performance of the school system and provide community-owned quality elementary education in the mission mode. It also envisages bridging of gender and social disparities at the elementary level. The Sarva Shiksha Abhiyan has a special focus on the educational needs of girls, SCs and STs and other children in difficult circumstances.

Objectives of Sarva Shiksha Abhiyan

- All children to be in schools, Education Guarantee Scheme Centres, alternative schools, by 2003;
- All children to complete five years of primary schooling by 2007;
- All children to complete eight years of schooling by 2010;
- Focus on elementary education of satisfactory quality with emphasis on education for life;
- Bridging all gender and social disparities at the primary stage by 2007 and at the upper primary level by 2010; and
- Universal retention by 2010.

Central Government's Assistance to States

The assistance under the programme of Sarva Shiksha Abhiyan was on a 85:15 sharing arrangement during the Ninth Plan, 75:25 sharing arrangement during the Tenth Plan and 50:50 sharing thereafter between the Central Government and the State Government except for 8 Northeast states, where 15 per cent of the state there met by Ministry of DONER for the two years 2005-06 and 2006-07.

Coverage: The programme covers the entire country with special focus on educational needs of girls, SCs/STs and other children in difficult circumstances. The programme seeks to open new schools in those places which do not have schooling facilities and strengthen existing school infrastructure through provision of additional class rooms, toilets, drinking water, maintenance grant and school improvement grant. SSA has a special focus on girls and children of weaker sections. A number of initiatives, including distribution of free textbooks, targeting these children is under the programme. The SSA also seeks to provide computer education even in the rural areas.

10. Education Guarantee Scheme and Alternative and Innovative Education

Education Guarantee Scheme and Alternative and Innovative Education (EGS and AIE) is an important component of Sarva Shiksha Abhiyan (SSA) to bring out-of-school children in the fold of Elementary Education. The scheme envisages that child-wise planning is undertaken for each out-of-school children.

EGS addresses the inaccessible habitation where there is no formal school within the radius of one km and at least 15-25 children of 6-14 years age group who are not going to school are available. In exceptional cases of remote habitations in hilly areas even for 20 children an EGS school can be opened.

Alternative Education interventions for specific categories of very deprived children e.g. child labour, street children, migrating children, working children, children living in difficult circumstances and older children in the 9+ age group especially adolescent girls are being supported under EGS and AIE all over the country.

A sizeable number of out-of-school children are in the habitations where schooling facility is available but these children either did not join the school or dropped out before completing their schooling. These children may not fit into the rigid formal system. To bring such children back to school, back to school camp and Bridge Courses strategies have been implemented. Bridge courses and back to school camps can be residential or non-residential depending upon the need of children.

5.2 QUALITY IMPROVEMENT IN SCHOOLS

During the 10th Five Year Plan, "Quality Improvement in Schools" was introduced as a composite centrally sponsored scheme having the following components: (i) National Population Education Project, (ii) Environmental Orientation to School Education, (iii) Improvement of Science Education in Schools, (iv) Introduction of Yoga in Schools, and (v) International Science Olympiads.

National Population Education Project (NPEP)

National Population Education Project was launched in April 1982 with the overarching objective of institutionalising population education in the school education and teacher education systems to contribute to the attainment of population and development goals of the country. Up to 2002, this was implemented as externally aided project which was fully funded by the United Nations Population Fund (UNFPA). It was being implemented in the University education and adult education sector as well.

UNFPA decided to support a concomitant Project focused on adolescent reproductive and sexual health (ARSH) from 2004.

Environmental Orientation to School Education

The National Policy on Education (NPE)-1986 provides that the protection of environment is a value which, along with certain other values, must form an integral part of curricula at all stages of education. To operationalise this noble objective, the mind and intellect of the students must be sensitised to the hazards inherent in nature upsetting the ecological balance in nature. This step inculcates awareness and respect among students for basic concepts relating to the conservation of environment.

To this end, a Centrally Sponsored Scheme "Environment Orientation to School Education" was initiated in 1988-89. The scheme envisages assistance to voluntary agencies for conduct of experimental and innovative programmes aimed at promoting integration of educational programmes in schools with local environmental conditions.

Improvement of Science Education in Schools

To improve the quality of science education and to promote the scientific temper as envisaged in the National Policy on Education, 1986, a Centrally Sponsored Scheme; "Improvement of Science Education in Schools" was initiated during 1987-88. Under the scheme financial assistance was being provided to States/UTs and voluntary agencies. While voluntary agencies were provided assistance for conducting experimental and innovative programmes States/Union Territories were assisted for provision of science kits to Upper Primary Schools, setting up of upgradation of science laboratories in Secondary/Senior Secondary Schools, Library facilities in Secondary/Senior Secondary Schools and Training of Science and Mathematics teachers.

One of the important components of this scheme was participation of Indian Students at school level in the International Science Olympiads, viz. International Mathematical Olympiad (since 1989), International Physics Olympiad (since 1998), International Chemistry Olympiad (since 1999) and International Biology Olympiad (since 2000).

Introduction of Yoga in Schools

Introduction of Yoga in schools was launched as a Centrally Sponsored

Scheme during 1989-90 to provide financial assistance to States/Union Territories/Non-Governmental Organisations. It aimed at giving central assistance for training and research, enrichment of library and construction/expansion of hostels for teacher trainees. It was being implemented through the concerned Departments of Education of States/UTs. It was transferred to NCERT w.e.f. April 2007. NCERT has initiated to review the Scheme in the light of National Curriculum Framework 2005.

International Science Olympiads

With an aim to identify and nurture talents in Mathematics, Physics, Chemistry and Biology at school level, and International Mathematical Olympiad (IMO), International Physics Olympiad (IPhO), International Chemistry Olympiad (IChO) and International Biology Olympiad (IBO) are held every year. India has been participating country in these Olympiads since 1989, 1998, 1999 and 2000, respectively. Each participating country is required to send a team comprising not more than 6 secondary students contestants to IMO, 5 secondary student contestants at IPhO, 4 contestants to IChO and 4 contestants to IBO apart from a Team Leader and a Deputy Team Leader. Since 2002 Indian team is also participating in international Olympiad in informatics.

Strengthening of Culture and Values in Education

The National Policy on Education, 1986 (revised in 1992) and its Programme of Action-1992 has laid considerable emphasis on value education by highlighting the need to make education a forceful tool for social and moral values.

To fulfil the objectives of the National Policy on Education, a Central Sector Scheme of Assistance for Strengthening of Culture and Values in Education is being implemented. Under this Scheme, financial assistance is given to Governmental and non-Governmental organisations, Panchayati Raj Institutions, etc., to the extent of 100 per cent of grant for the project proposals approved, subject to a ceiling, for strengthening cultural and value education from pre-primary education system to higher education including technical and management education.

Scholarships

The Ministry of Human Resource Development operates a Centrally Sponsored Scheme viz. National Merit Scholarship Scheme through States/UTs, under which 100 per cent financial assistance is provided to meritorious students from rural areas studying in classes IX and X. Besides scholarship is also provided to all the meritorious students on state-wise merit, including students from rural areas, studying from the post-metric to the post-graduate level.

The Government provides scholarship to Indian scholar for Post-Graduate/Research/Post-Doctoral studies abroad on the basis of offers received from foreign Government under the various Cultural/Educational Exchange Programme. The details of offers and other conditions are given wide publicity in the leading newspapers while inviting applications for scholarship and are available on Department's website www.education.nic.in. The amount and other facilities provided by foreign governments varies from country to country and from time-to-time.

5.3 TEACHER EDUCATION RESTRUCTURING AND REORGANISATION

Objectives: As envisaged in the NPE and Programme of Action (POA), 1996, a Central Scheme of Restructuring and Reorganisation of Teachers Education was taken up in 1987 for the following purposes:

(i) Creating a viable institutional infrastructure of teacher education.

(ii) Building up an academic and technical base for orientation, training and continuous upgrading of knowledge, competence and pedagogical skills of elementary school teachers in the country.

Components: 1. Establishment of District Institute of Education & Training (DIETs) by upgradation of existing Elementary Teacher Education Institutions (ETEIs) wherever possible, and establishment of new DIET where necessary.

2. Upgradation of selected Secondary Teacher Education Institutions (STETIs) into:

(a) Colleges of Teacher Education (CTEs), and

(b) Institutes of Advanced Study in Education (IASEs).

3. Strengthening of State Council of Educational Research and Training (SCERTs).

The Scheme was revised in 2003 and the revised guidelines were issued in January 2004. The main objectives of the Teacher Education Scheme are as follows:

1. Speedy completion of DIET/CTE/IASE/SCERT projects sanctioned but not completed up to the end of the IX Plan period.
2. Making DIETs, IASEs sanctioned (and SCERTs strengthened) up to the IX Plan period, optimally functional and operational.
3. Sanction and implementation of fresh DIET/CTE/IASE/SCERT projects to the extent necessary.
4. Improvement in the quality of programmes to be undertaken by DIETs, etc. especially those of pre-service and in-service training, so as to enable them to effectively play their nodal role of

improving quality of elementary and secondary education in their respective jurisdiction, as measured in terms of levels of learner achievements.

Criteria for setting up of DIETs/District Resource Centre (DRC) are:

1. One DIET for each district having a minimum of 2,500 teachers. If there is an existing Government ETEI in the district, it would be upgraded into a DIET. If no Government ETEI exists in the district, a new institution (DIET) will be established.

2. District Resource Centres in districts with less than 2,500 teachers. If a Government ETEI exists in the district, it would be upgraded into a DRC. Otherwise, a new DRC would be established in which case it would not conduct pre-service course.

3. If in a district with more than 2,500 teachers, State Government wishes to establish a DRC in preference to a DIET, it would be able to do so.

5.4 ADULT EDUCATION

National Literacy Mission

The National Literacy Mission set up in May 1988 aims to attain a sustainable threshold level of 75 per cent literacy by 2007 by imparting functional literacy to non-literates in the age group of 15-35 years, which is the productive and reproductive age group and constitutes a major segment of the work force. Apart from predetermined levels of reading, writing and numeracy with comprehension, functional literacy includes imbibing values of national integration, conservation of environment, women's equality, observance of small family norms, etc. Literacy, as enunciated in NLM, is not an end in itself but has to be an active and potent instrument of change ensuring achievement of these social objectives and creation of a learning society. The acquisition of functional literacy results in empowerment and a definite improvement in the quality of life.

The *Total Literacy Campaign* (TLC) is the principal strategy of NLM for eradication of illiteracy. These campaigns are area-specific, time-bound, participative, cost-effective and outcome oriented. They are implemented through Zila Saksharata Samities (district level literacy committees) as independent and autonomous bodies, having due representation of all sections of society. Apart from imparting functional literacy, TLC also disseminates a 'basket' of other socially relevant messages such as need for enrolment and retention of children in schools, immunisation, propagation of small family norms, women's equality and empowerment, peace and communal harmony, etc. These literacy campaigns generated a demand for primary education. The basic literacy skills acquired by millions of non-literates are at best fragile. There is a greater possibility of neo-literates regressing into partial or total illiteracy unless special efforts are continued to consolidate, sustain and possibly enhance their literacy levels. The National Literacy Mission aims at ensuring that the Total Literacy Campaigns and the Post-literacy Programmes successfully move on to Continuing Education, which provide life-long learning.

The *Continuing Education* Scheme provides a learning continuum to the efforts of Total Literacy and Post-Literacy Programmes in the country. The main thrust is on providing further learning opportunities to neo-literates by setting up of Continuing Education Centres (CECs) which provide area-specific, need-based opportunities for basic literacy, upgradation of literacy skills, pursuit of alternative educational programmes, vocational skill and also to promote social and occupational development. The scheme also undertakes a number of important programmes such as — Equivalency Programme facilitating the participants to acquire or upgrade their vocational skills and take up income-generating activities; quality of life improvement programme to equip learners and the community with essential knowledge; attitude, values and skills to raise their standards of living; and Individual Interest Promotion Programme providing opportunities for learners to participate and learn about their individually chosen social, health, physical, cultural, and artistic interests. The programmes of residual illiteracy are also being taken up to address the requirements of geographically remote regions and segments of population requiring special focus, particularly SCs/STs/Women. So far, about 330 districts have been covered under the Continuing Education Programme.

Non-Governmental Organisations: The National Literacy Mission (NLM) fully recognises the vast potential of NGOs in furthering its objectives and has taken measures to strengthen its partnership with NGOs and has assigned them an active promotional role in the literacy movement. Apart from imparting literacy, the NGOs provide academic and technical resource support through experimental and innovative programmes.

The State Resource Centres (SRCs) managed by NGOs provide academic and technical resource support in the form of training material preparation, extension activities, innovative projects, research studies and evaluation, etc. At present, there are 26 SRCs.

Special Interventions for Female Literacy: As per Census, 2001, 47 districts in the country had a female literacy rate below 30 per cent. Hence, dealing with low female literacy is of immense concern to the National Literacy Mission and it was decided to target the 47 low female literacy districts for improvement. Most of the these districts are concentrated in the States of Uttar Pradesh, Bihar, Orissa and Jharkhand.

Projects for Residual Illiteracy: Although the Total Literacy Campaigns took the form of mass movement and spread throughout the country in many cases a number of campaigns stagnated due to natural calamites, lack of political will, etc. Despite success of literacy phase, there are still pockets of residual illiteracy and low female literacy.

Special Literacy Drive: The Council of the NLMA in its meeting held in April 2005 identified 150 districts which had the lowest literacy rates in the country for launching a special literacy drive, with special focus on the minority groups, persons belonging to scheduled castes, scheduled tribes, women and other backward sections of the society by drawing up implementation strategies suited to the specific needs of the groups, sections of the society or region.

Jan Shikshan Sansthan: The objective of the Jan Shikshan Sansthan (JSS) is educational, vocational and occupational development of the socio-economically backward and educationally disadvantaged groups of urban/rural population particularly neo-literates, semi-literates, SCs, STs, women and girls, slum dwellers, migrant workers, etc.

Directorate of Adult Education: The Central Directorate of Adult Education provides academic and technical resource support to National Literacy Mission. It has been playing an important role in the development of a network of resource support, particularly production of prototype teaching/learning materials/media software and harnessing of all kinds of media for realising the objectives of NLM.

6

Education of the Deprived

Constitutional Provisions and Their Implementation

6.1 EDUCATION OF SCHEDULED CASTES (SCs)

Article 46 of the Constitution states that, "The State shall promote, with special care, the education and economic interests of the weaker sections of the people, and in particular of the Scheduled Castes and Scheduled Tribes, and shall protect them from social injustice and all forms of social exploitation". Articles 330, 332, 335, 338 to 342 and the entire Fifth and Sixth Schedules of the Constitution deal with the special provisions for implementation of the objectives set forth in Article 46. These provisions need to be fully utilised for the benefit of the weaker sections of our society.

Article 330: It relates to reservation of seats for Scheduled Castes and Scheduled Tribes in the House of People.

Article 332: It refers to the reservation of SCs and STs in the Legislative Assemblies of the States.

Article 335: It is concerned with the claims of SCs and STs to services and posts.

Article 338: It provides for the Constitution of National Commission for Scheduled Castes.

Article 339: It deals with the control of the Union over the administration of Scheduled Areas and the Welfare of the Scheduled Tribes.

Article 340: It provides for the appointment of the Commission to investigate the conditions of backward classes.

Articles 341 and *342*: These relate to the declaration of Castes as SCs and STs.

All these articles have a great bearing on the empowerment i.e. education and welfare of the SCs and STs.

The Ministries which take several steps for the education and welfare of the SCs. are:

(i) The Ministry of Human Resource Development, Government of India.

(ii) The Ministry of Social Justice and Empowerment.

(iii) The Ministry for Tribal Areas.

Major Steps Taken for the Education of SCs and STs

1. *Relaxation of Norms*. The Departments of Elementary Education and Literacy and Secondary and Higher Education have relaxed norms for opening of primary/middle schools.

2. *Abolition of Tuition Fee*: Tuition fee has been abolished in all States in Government schools at least up to the upper primary level. Most of the States have abolished tuition fees for SC and ST students up to the senior secondary level.

3. *Incentives:* Incentives like free textbooks, uniform, stationery, school bags, etc. are provided for the students.

4. *Special Provisions under SSA*: These provisions are discussed separately.

5. *Pre-Matric Scholarships for Children of those engaged in Unclean Occupation*: Under the Scheme, the Children of families engaged in unclean occupations such as scavenging, flaying and tanning are assisted to pursue education up to the matriculation level. The scholarship is provided through State Governments and Union Territory Administrations. Central assistance is provided to the State Governments on 50:50 basis and to the Union Territory Administration on 100 per cent basis over and above their committed liability. Students amongst the target groups with disabilities are also assisted. There is no income ceiling prescribed under the scheme.

The scheme provides scholarship of Rs. 40 per month in classes I to V, Rs. 60 per month in classes VI to VIII and Rs. 75 per month in classes IX to X in respect of day scholars; for hostellers Rs. 300 per month in classes III to VIII and Rs. 375 per month in classes IX to X.

The duration of scholarship in an academic year is ten months. The Day Scholars and hostellers are eligible for ad-hoc grant of Rs. 550 and Rs. 600 per student per annum respectively.

Post-Matric Scholarships for SC Students: Under this scheme, financial assistance is provided to Scheduled Caste students for pursuing studies beyond matriculation in recognised institutions. The assistance includes maintenance allowance for various categories of courses, reimbursement of compulsory non-refundable fee charged by the institutions and other allowances such as study tour charges, thesis typing/printing charges and book grant, revisions of income ceiling to Rs. one lakh per annum for eligibility Scholarship which is disbursed through respective State Governments and UT Administrations.

The scheme provides for 100 per Central assistance to the State Governments and UT Administrations over and above the perspective committed liability of the States/UTs. The committed liability of the North Eastern States has, however, been dispensed with.

6. *Rajiv Gandhi National Fellowship Scheme*: A new Scheme named Rajiv Gandhi National Fellowship (RGNF) for Scheduled Caste Students was introduced during the financial year 2005-06. Fellowships, in the form of financial assistance, are provided to students belonging to Scheduled Castes to pursue higher studies leading to award of M.Phil and PhD degree.

A student, belonging to Scheduled Caste registered in a regular and full time M.Phil/PhD course in a University/Academic institution will be eligible for the fellowship. The fellowships will be on the same scale as that of the University Grants Commission (UGC) Junior Research Fellowships. The scheme is being implemented through the University Grants Commission.

7. *Upgradation of Merit for SC Students*: The main objective of the scheme is to upgrade the merit of Scheduled Caste students by providing them with facilities for all-round development through education in residential schools. The scheme provides for 100 per cent Central assistance to States/UTs. for arrangement of remedial and special coaching for SC students studying in class IX to XII. Financial assistance is provided to students as package grant.

8. *National Overseas Scholarship and Passage Grants for Higher Education*: Under this scheme assistance is provided to meritorious students for pursuing higher studies of Masters level courses, PhD and Post-Doctoral Research Programmes abroad in specified fields like Engineering, Technology and Sciences, only. The awardees were permitted to undertake research/teaching assistantship. Financial assistance under the scheme is provided for a maximum period of four years for PhD research, for 3 years for Master's Programme Students whose family income exceeds Rs. 18,000 per month are not eligible for assistance and only one child of the same parents/guardians is eligible to get benefit under the scheme. The prospective awardees should not be more than 35 years of age.

9. *Coaching and Allied Scheme for Weaker Sections including SCs, OBCs and Minorities*: The scheme aimed to equip aspiring students for preparing them for various competitive exams. Aspiring students take their guidance and coaching from the centers run by State Governments/UTs., Universities and NGOs.

10. *Hostels for Scheduled Caste Boys and Girls*: The objective of the Scheme is to provide hostel facilities to SC Boys and Girls studying in middle schools, higher secondary schools, colleges and universities. The financial assistance is provided for construction of hostels. The maintenance of hostels, boarding and lodging of students, however rests with the respective States/UTs. The Scheme provides for release of Central Assistance to State Governments on 50:50 matching share basis and 100% to UTs. and also 90% to Central Universities. Other Universities can also get Central Assistance up to 45% and the remaining amount has to be provided by their respective States (45%). The NGOs also get assistance on the basis of 45:45:10 through their States/UTs. for extension of their existing hostels.

Provisions under SSA

1. *Special Provisions*: (i) Focus on girls especially belonging to SC/ST communities and minority groups.

(ii) Back to school camps for out of school girls.

(iii) Free textbooks for girls, SC/ST students.

(iv) Special coaching/remedial classes for girls SC/ST children and a congenial learning environment.

(v) Teachers' sensitisation programmes to promote equitable learning opportunities.

(vi) Special focus for innovative projects related to girls' education, SC/ST children.

(vii) Recruitment of 50 per cent female teachers.

2. *National Programme for Education of Girls at Elementary Level* (*NPEGEL*): The NPEGEL under the existing scheme of Sarva Shiksha Abhiyan (SSA) provides additional components for education of girls from under privileged/disadvantaged sections of the society at the elementary level. The Scheme is being implemented in Educationally Backward Blocks (EBBs) where the level of rural female literacy is less than the national average and the gender gap is above the national average, as well as in blocks of districts that have at least 5 per cent SC/ST population and where SC/ST female literacy is below 10 per cent. (based on 1991 census).

3. *Mahila Samakhya* (*MS*): MS addresses traditional gender imbalances in educational access and achievement. This involves enabling women (especially from socially and economically disadvantaged and marginalised groups) to address and deal with problems of isolation and lack of self-confidence, oppressive social customs and struggle for survival, all of which inhibit their empowerment.

4. *District Primary Education Programme* (*DPEP*): The thrust of the scheme is on disadvantaged groups like girls, SCs/STs, working children, urban deprived children, disabled children, etc. There are specific strategies for girls and SCs/STs; however, physical targets are fixed, in an integrated manner including coverage of these groups as well. According to a study by NIEPA, schools in DPEP districts had more than 60 per cent students belonging to SC/ST communities.

5. *Kasturba Gandhi Balika Vidyalayas*: Under the scheme of Kasturba Gandhi Balika Vidyalayas, 750 residential schools are being set up in difficult areas with boarding facilities at elementary level for girls belonging, predominantly, to the SC, ST, OBC and minorities. The scheme would be applicable only in those identified Educationally Backward Blocks (EBBs) where, as per census data 2001, the rural female literacy is below the national average and gender gap in literacy more than the national average. Among these blocks, schools may be set up in areas with

concentration of tribal population, with low female literacy and/or a large number of girls out of school.

6. *Shiksha Karmi Project* (*SKP*): SKP aims at universalisation and qualitative improvement of primary education in remote, arid and socio-economically backward villages in Rajasthan with primary attention to girls. It is noteworthy that in Shiksha Karmi Schools, most of the students are from SCs, STs and OBCs.

7. *Jan Shikshan Sansthan* (*JSS*): The Scheme of JSS or Institute of People's Education is a polyvalent or multifaceted adult education programme aimed at improving the vocational skill and the quality of life of the beneficiaries. The objective of the scheme is educational, vocational and occupational development of the socio-economically backward and educationally disadvantaged groups of urban/rural population particularly neo-literates, semi-literates, SCs, STs, women and girls, slum dwellers, migrant workers etc.

Literacy campaigns have had an enormous impact on other social sectors. The campaigns have served the cause of promoting equity and social justice in society and fostering of a scientific temper and a sense of belonging to India's great composite culture and consciousness of unity in diversity.

8. *Mid-Day Meal Scheme*: The Mid-Day Meal scheme is a successful incentive programme. It covers all students including SCs/STs of primary classes in all Government, local body and Government aided schools in the country with the aim to improve enrolment, attendance and retention while simultaneously impacting on the nutritional status of the children.

9. *Central Institute of Indian Languages* (*CIIL*): The Central Institute of Indian Languages, Mysore has a scheme of development of Indian Languages through research, developing manpower and production of materials in modern Indian languages including tribal languages. The Institute has worked in more than 90 tribal and border languages.

10. *Kendriya Vidyalayas* (*KVs*): 15 per cent and 7.5 per cent seats are reserved for SCs and STs respectively in fresh admissions. No tuition fee is charged from Scheduled Caste and Scheduled Tribe students up to class XII.

11. *Navodaya Vidyalayas* (*NVs*): Reservation of seats in favour of children belonging to SCs and STs is provided in proportion to their population in the concerned district provided that no such reservation will be less than the national average of 22.5 per cent (15 per cent for SCs and 7.50 per cent for STs) and a maximum of 50 per cent for both the categories (SCs & STs) taken together. These reservations are interchangeable and are over and above the students selected under open merit.

12. *National Institute of Open Schooling* (*NIOS*): The SC/ST students are given concessions in admission fees to the extent of Rs. 200/- for bridge

courses, Rs. 250/- for secondary courses and Rs. 300/- for senior secondary courses.

Under the Scheme of Strengthening of Boarding and Hostel Facilities for Girl Students of Secondary & Higher Secondary Schools cent per cent financial assistance is given to Voluntary Organisations to improve enrolment of adolescent girls belonging to Rural areas and weaker sections. Preference is given to educationally backward districts particularly those pre-dominantly inhabited by SCs/STs and educationally backward minorities.

13. *National Merit Scholarship Scheme*: The National Scholarship Scheme and Scheme of Scholarship at the Secondary Stage for Talented Children from Rural Areas are in existence since 1961-62 and 1971-72, respectively. These have been merged and a new scheme entitled 'National Merit Scholarship Scheme' has been framed for implementation with the revised provisions from 2004-05. The objective of the National Merit Scholarship Scheme is to support talented students and encourage them to excel academically in studies by giving recognition and financial assistance at post-matric level on state wise merit basis and also separately to talented and meritorious students in rural areas for Classes IX to X for all categories. The revised rate of scholarship varies from Rs. 250/- to Rs. 750/- p.m., depending on the level of education, and course of study. The scheme is implemented through the State Governments.

14. *National Council for Educational Research & Training* (*NCERT*): NCERT focuses on the development of textbooks, workbooks, teacher guides, supplementary reading materials, evaluation of textbooks, vocational education educational technology, examination reforms, support to Sarva Shiksha Abhiyan, education of educationally disadvantaged groups.

NCERT operates the National Talent Search Scheme for pursuing courses in science and social sciences up to doctoral level and in professional courses like medicine and engineering up to the second-degree level subject to fulfillment of the conditions. Out of 1,000 scholarships, 150 scholarships are reserved for SC students and 75 scholarships for ST students.

15. *National Institute of Educational Planning & Administration* (*NIEPA*) (*Now known as NUEPA*): Educational development of Scheduled Castes and Scheduled Tribes is an area of major concern of NUEPA. It carries out a number of studies relating to educational programmes and schemes for scheduled castes and scheduled Tribes. It has also been generating material relating to educational institutions and development of Scheduled Caste and Scheduled Tribe students.

16. *University Grants Commission* (*UGC*): UGC provides financial assistance to universities/deemed universities for the establishment of

SC/ST Cells in the Universities to ensure effective implementation of reservation policy for SCs and STs. The UGC has established SC/ST Cells in many Universities including Central Universities to ensure proper implementation of the reservation policy. The Standing Committee on SCs/STs monitors and reviews the work undertaken by the universities/colleges.

17. As per the reservation policy, UGC has earmarked 15 per cent and 7.50 per cent reservation for SCs and STs respectively in appointments, both in teaching and non- teaching posts, admissions, hostel accommodation, etc., in universities/colleges, professional and technical educational institutions administered by the Central Government. State universities follow reservation policy as prescribed by respective state governments. The Commission has been issuing guidelines/directives/ instructions from time-to-time for implementing reservation policy of the Government of India.

18. Apart from reservation, there is also relaxation in the minimum qualifying marks for admission for SC/ST candidates.

19. UGC has been implementing the programme of Career Orientation to Education (vocationalisation of education) to ensure that the graduates have knowledge, skills and attitudes for gainful employment in the wage sectors in general, and self-employment in particular for all, including SCs/STs.

20. UGC provides financial assistance for Remedial Coaching to SC/ST students. It provides financial assistance to the existing coaching centres to prepare SC/ST candidates for the National Eligibility Test (NET) conducted by UGC/CSIR.

21. Commission provides financial assistance for extension activities. Under the scheme, all groups of the society are covered, including SCs/STs.

22. In order to contribute towards social equity and socio-economic mobility of the under privileged sections of the society UGC has introduced remedial coaching scheme at UG/PG level. The main objectives of the scheme are: (i) to improve the academic skills and linguistic proficiency of the students in various subjects; (ii) to raise the level of comprehension of basic subjects so as to provide a strong foundation for further academic work; (iii) to strengthen their knowledge, skills and attitudes in the subjects where quantitative and qualitative techniques and laboratory work are involved; and (iv) to improve the overall performance of these students in the examination.

23. Commission has created a Central Pool Database of eligible SC/ST candidates and recommends their candidature for teaching positions in order to fulfil the prescribed reservation quota in universities and colleges.

24. Periodic meetings of Registrars of Central Universities are organised to review the implementation of reservation policy in the Central Universities.

25. Commission has also constituted a Special Monitoring Committee, which reviews the functioning of existing Cells.

26. *Community Polytechnics*: The Scheme of Community Polytechnics undertakes rural/community development activities through application of science and technology, in its proximity. It provides platform for transfer of appropriate technologies to rural masses/local communities. Preference is given in training to rural youths, SCs, STs, women, school drop-outs and other disadvantaged groups and helps them to obtain need based gainful employment. The scheme of Community Polytechnics has been in operation in selected diploma level institutions since 1978-79. It applies science and technology through skill oriented non-formal training, technology transfer and technical support services.

27. *Engineering Colleges*: The higher educational institutions administered by the Central Government including IITs, IIMs, Regional Engineering Colleges, etc., provide reservation to the extent of 15 per cent and 7.5 per cent for SCs and STs students respectively. Apart from reservation there is also relaxation in the minimum qualifying marks for admission for SC/ST students. Seats are also reserved in hostels. However, in institutions run by the State Governments, the reservation percentages varies as per the State Government's policy.

6.2 EDUCATION OF STs

The Ministry of Tribal Affairs is primarily responsible for the education of the ST students.

Major Schemes

1. *Boys'/Girls' Hostels for Scheduled Tribes* (*Centrally Sponsored Scheme*): The scheme of Girls' Hostels, which started in the Third Plan, and another scheme for the construction of Boys' Hostels was in operation since 1989-90 is a useful instrument for spreading education among ST Girls, whose literacy still stands at 18.19 per cent as per 1991 Census as against the general female literacy of 29.23 per cent. The scheme of Boys' Hostels was merged with the scheme of Girls' Hostels in the Tenth Five Year Plan. Under the scheme, Central assistance is given to States/UTs. for construction of new hostel buildings and/or extension of existing hostels. This is a Centrally Sponsored Scheme where the cost of the construction of the hostel building is equally shared between the Centre and the State in the ratio of 50:50. In case of UTs., the Central Government bears the entire cost of the building. The cost of construction is based on the State PWD schedule of rates or local CPWD schedule of rates, whichever is lower. Maintenance of the hostel is the responsibility of the concerned States/UTs. The number of seats in a hostel is limited and is generally up to 100. The

hostels are for ST girls in middle and high schools, colleges and universities.

2. *Boys, Hostel for Scheduled Tribes* (*Centrally Sponsored Scheme*): The objectives, items and conditions as well as the pattern of assistance of this scheme for same as that of the scheme for Girls Hostels. The scheme is in operation since 1989-90.

3. *Establishment of Ashram Schools in Tribal Sub-Plan Area*: The scheme of Ashram Schools, a Centrally Sponsored Scheme, was launched in 1990-91 with the objective to extend facilities like the establishment of residential schools for STs in an environment conducive to learning to increase literacy rates among the tribal students and to bring them at par with the other population of the country. The funding for the scheme, with the State, is done on matching (50-50) basis, while cent per cent assistance is given to UTs.

4. *Upgradation of Merit of ST Students*: The objective of this Central Sector scheme is to upgrade the merit of ST students by providing them remedial and special coaching in classes IX to XII. While the remedial coaching aims at removing deficiencies in various subjects, the special coaching is provided with a view to prepare the students for competitive examinations for seeking entry into professional courses like Engineering and Medical disciplines. The scheme provides for 100 per cent Central assistance to the States/UTs. A package grant of Rs. 15,000 per student per year is provided and the States/UTs. are not required to bear any financial burden. The students with disabilities amongst STs receive specified special allowances like reader's allowance, escort's allowance, etc.

5. *Post-Matric Scholarships for Scheduled Tribes Students*: The objective of the scheme is to provide financial assistance to students belonging to STs pursuing Post-Matriculation recognised courses in recognised institutions. The scheme covers professional, technical, non-professional and non-technical courses at various levels. It also includes correspondence courses including distance and continuing education and is implemented by the State Government and UT Administrations, covering 100% Central Assistance over and above the committed liability which is required to be borne by them from their own budgetary provisions.

6. *Vocational Training in Tribal Areas*: The main aim of this scheme is to develop the skill of the tribal youth in order to gain employment/self-employment opportunities. This scheme was introduced in 1992-93 as Central Sector Scheme and implemented through the State Governments/UT Administrations, Institutions or Organisations set up by Government as autonomous body educational and other institutions like local bodies and cooperative societies and Non-Governmental Organisations. The capacity of each vocational training center is 100 with hostel facility for 50. Each center caters to five vocational courses in the

traditional skills depending upon the employment potential of the area. Each tribal boy/girl is trained in two trades of his/her choice, the course in each trade being of three months duration. Each trainee is attached at the end of six months to a Master Craftsman in a semi-urban area for a period of six months to learn his/her skill by practical experience, the practical experience of each trade being of three months duration. There is a provision for monthly stipend and for raw material for the trainees.

7. *Education of Girls in Low Literacy Pockets*: The scheme envisages setting up of residential educational complex as from first to fifth standard. This scheme was launched in 1993-94 with the objective of raising the literacy level of tribal females in 48 identified tribal districts in eight States with female literacy below two per cent. This scheme was revised in July 1998 and now covers 136 districts having female literacy of less than 10 per cent in 14 States.

8. *Grants in Aid to Voluntary Organisations*: The Ministry gives Grant in Aid to voluntary organisations working for the welfare of STs for projects like residential schools, hostels, medical units, computer training units, shorthand, and typing training unit, *balwadis*/crèches (in areas not covered by the ICDS programme), libraries and audio-visual units. The grant is generally restricted to 90 per cent of the approved total cost of the project and the balance 10 per cent is borne by the grantee organisations.

9. *Rajiv Gandhi National Fellowship* (*RGNF*): The Ministry of Tribal Affairs has launched a new Central Sector Scheme, namely Rajiv Gandhi National Fellowship (RGNF) of the initiative of the Planning Commission from the Year 2005-06. The scheme is for providing fellowship to ST students to enable them to pursue higher studies such as M.Phil and PhD. Total number of scholarships are 667 per year and maximum duration of the scholarship is 5 years.

10. *National Overseas Scholarship Scheme for Scheduled Tribes* (*Non-Plan*): The scheme provides for financial assistance to meritorious students for pursuing higher studies abroad in specified fields of Master level courses, PhD. and Post-Doctoral research programmes, in the field of Engineering, Technology and Science for Scheduled Tribes, Denotified, Nomadic and Semi-nomadic tribes. The selected candidates are provided the cost of tuition and other educational fees charged by the foreign university, etc., maintenance and other grants along with travel expenses. In addition passage grants are also available to candidates belonging to ST who are in receipt of merit scholarship for postgraduate studies, research or training abroad (excluding attending seminars, workshops, conferences) from a foreign government/organisations or under any other scheme where cost of passage is not provided. The scheme of NOS has been revised in 2004-05.

The scheme provides financial assistance to meritorious ST students for pursuing higher studies abroad in specified fields of Master level courses,

PhD. and Post-Doctoral research programmes, in the field of Engineering Technology and Science.

11. *Scheme of Top Class Education for Scheduled Tribe Students*: The Ministry of Tribal Affairs has introduced a new scheme of Top Class Education of ST students from 2007-08 with the objective of encouraging meritorious ST students for pursuing studies at degree and post-degree level in any of the selected list of institutes of excellence, in which the scholarship scheme would be operative. There are 127 top-rated institutes approved under the scheme in both the Government and private sectors covering the field of management, medicine, engineering, law and commercial courses. Each institute has been allocated five awards, with a ceiling of total 635 scholarships per year.

6.3 RESERVATION OF SEATS FOR SCs, STs AND OBCs IN CENTRAL EDUCATIONAL INSTITUTIONS

Constitutional Provisions

Part IV of the Constitution, containing the Directive Principles of State Policy, in Article 46, lays down that the State shall promote with special care the educational and economic interests of the weaker sections of the people, and, in particular, of the Scheduled Castes and the Scheduled Tribes, and shall protect them from social injustice. Access to education is of utmost importance in insuring advancement of persons belonging to the Scheduled Castes, the Scheduled Tribes, and the socially and educationally backward classes of citizens, who are also referred to as the Other Backward Classes (OBCs).

The Central Educational Institutions (Reservation in Short Title Admission) Act, 2006

The Act provides for the reservation in admission of the students belonging to the Scheduled Castes, the Scheduled Tribes and the Other Backward Classes of citizens to certain central educational institutions established, maintained or aided by the Central Government and for matters connected therewith or incidental thereto.

The reservation of seats in admission and its extent in a Central Educational Institution is to be provided in the following manner, namely:

(i) out of the annual permitted strength in each branch of study or faculty, fifteen per cent, shall be reserved for the Scheduled Castes.

(ii) out of the annual permitted strength in each branch of study or faculty, seven and one-half per cent seats shall be reserved for the Scheduled Tribes.

(iii) out of the annual permitted strength in each branch of study or faculty twenty seven per cent seats shall be reserved for the Other Backward Classes.

Act not to Apply in Certain Cases

The provisions of Section 3 of this Act shall not apply to:

(a) a Central Educational Institution established in the tribal areas referred to in the Sixth Schedule to the Constitution.

(b) the institutions of excellence, research institutions, institutions of national and strategic importance specified in the Schedule to this Act:

Provided that the Central Government may as and when considered necessary, by notification in the Official Gazette, amend the Schedule;

(c) a Minority Educational Institution as defined in this Act;

(d) a course or programme at high levels of specialisation, including at the post-doctoral level, within any branch of study or faculty, which the Central Government may, in consultation with the appropriate authority, specify.

Mandatory Increase of Seats

(1) Notwithstanding anything contained in clause (iii) of Section 3 and in any other law for the time being in force, every Central Educational Institution shall, with the prior approval of the appropriate authority, increase the number of seats in a branch of study or faculty over and above its annual permitted strength so that the number of seats, excluding those reserved for the persons belonging to the Scheduled Castes, the Scheduled Tribes and the Other Backward Classes, is not less than the number of such seats available for the academic session immediately preceding the date of the coming into force of this Act.

(2) Where, on a representation by any Central Educational Institution, the Central Government, in consultation with the appropriate authority, is satisfied that for reasons of financial, physical or academic limitation or in order to maintain the standards of education, the annual permitted strength in any branch of study or faculty of such institution cannot be increased for the academic session following the commencement of this Act, it may permit, by notification in the Official Gazette, such institution to increase the annual permitted strength over a maximum period of three years beginning with the academic session following the commencement of this Act; and then, the extent of reservation for the Other Backward Classes as provided in clause (iii) of Section 3 shall be limited for that academic session in such manner that the number of seats available to the Other Backward Classes for each academic session are commensurate with the increase in the permitted strength for each year.

Implementation of the Act

The Office Memorandum, 20th April, 2008 of the Government of India,

Ministry of Human Resource Development, Department of Higher Education to the implementation of reservation in admission.

The implementation of reservation in admission under the Central Educational Institutions (Reservation in Admissions) Act, 2006 [No. 5 of 2006] in respect of persons belonging to the socially and educationally backward classes (OBCs) had been 'stayed' by the Hon'ble Supreme Court of India while hearing Writ Petition (Civil) No. 265 and a bunch of other writ petitions. The Apex Court finally disposed of the petitions on the 10th April, 2008, upholding the constitutional validity of the 93rd Amendment [Article 15(5)] of the Constitution in so far as the Central Educational Institutions, established, maintained or aided by the Central Government are concerned. The court also upheld the CEI Act, 2006, with the directions that the OBCs shall not include socially advanced persons (commonly known as the "creamy layer"). Thus, all CEIs other than those mentioned in the Schedule of the CEI Act, had to implement the policy of reservation of 27 per cent of seats for the OBCs apart from 15 per cent seats for the SCs and 7.5 per cent for the STs from the academic session commencing 2008, in accordance with the phasing of the expansion of capacity necessitated in order to ensure that the seats available in the unreserved category are not reduced.

The Office Memorandum clarified the process of implementation of reservation for the OBCs as given below:

(i) The policy of reservation for the OBCs under the Central Educational Institutions Act is to be implemented from the forthcoming academic session itself.

(ii) This is applicable to all the CEIs, exceptions being only those institutions of excellence, research institutions of national and strategic importance specified in the Schedule to the CEI Act (copy of which is enclosed).

(iii) The policy of reservation for the OBCs/SCs & STs under the CEI Act is applicable to all programmes/courses of study at the undergraduate, graduate, post-graduate levels, etc. except courses or programmes at high levels of specialisation, including at the post-doctoral level within any branch of study which the Central Government in consultation with the appropriate statutory authority (UGC/BCI/MCI/AICTE, etc.) may specify. This is to reiterate that there shall be no exemption from the policy of reservation except where the Central Government so specifies a course or programme covered under clause (d) of Section 4 of the Act.

(iv) The reservation for the OBCs and SCs/STs under the CEI Act shall not apply to minority educational institutions as defined in Section 2 (f) of the Act as well as on CEIs established in areas coming under 6th Schedule of the Constitution.

(v) The Central Government is reportedly taking steps to ensure that CEIs are not put to difficulties in phasing of admissions under Section 6 of the Act, due to the deferment of reservations in admissions from the academic session in calendar year 2007, owing to the 'stay orders' of the Supreme Court.

(vi) Each Central Educational Institution shall ensure that from among candidates belonging to the OBCs applying for admission against the seats reserved for the OBC category, information is collected from the candidates for exercising due vigilance, so that no candidate belonging to the "creamy layer" is given the benefit of reservation for the OBCs.

(vii) In order to identify and exclude candidates belonging to the "creamy layer" the criteria of exclusion/rules of exclusion have been provided in OM No. 36012/22/93-(SCT), dated 8th September, 1993 of the Ministry of Personnel, Public Grievance and Pension, Department of Personnel and Training as amended by that Department vide OM No. 36033/3/2004-Estt. (Res) dated 9th March, 2004 and any other modifications that may take place from time-to-time in this regard.

(viii) The Socially and Educationally Backward Classes/OBCs who are eligible for availing the benefits of reservation is to be ascertained from the Central lists of SEBCs/OBCs as per Resolution No. 12011/68/93-DCC (C) of the Ministry of Welfare (now the Ministry of Social Justice & Empowerment) as modified from time-to-time by that Ministry based on the advice of the National Commission for Backward Classes (NCBC).

(ix) CEIs which have completed the process of admission test and selection of candidates in the SC, ST and unreserved categories, should identify the 'creamy layer' on the basis of the above mentioned information from among the successful waitlisted candidates belonging to the OBCs as per the Central List and, thereafter, offer admission to eligible candidates. For the purpóse of identification, candidates one required to furnish information on each of the criteria as per the prevailing rule of exclusion of the socially advanced persons (creamy layer).

For an updated list of state-wise OBCs eligible for availing the benefit of reservation, one can refer to the list maintained by the NCBC at its website http://ncbc.nic.in/backward-classes/index.html. one may also access information in respect of the creamy layer at http://ncbc.nic.in/html/creamylayer.html and for the clarifications issued by the Department of Personnel & Training on the definition of creamy layer and income criteria at http://persmin.gov.in/WriteData/WMS/ScanDocument/36033_5_2004_01A pril2005.htm. The Supreme Court judgements are also available at the NIC website http://www.judis.nic/supremecourt/CaseResi.aspx.

(x) Each CEI is also authorised to fix cut off marks for admission/selection through admission tests, etc. for the OBC candidates with such differential from the cut-off marks for the unreserved category as each institution may deem appropriate for maintaining the standards of education and at the same time ensuring that sufficient number of eligible OBC candidates are available in keeping with the directions/observations of the Hon'ble Supreme Court of India in this regard. This authorisation by the Central Government to the CEIs to fix the cut-off marks is in compliance with the Apex Court's direction asking the Central Government to examine the feasibility of determining such cut-off marks. The Central Government believes that each CEI would ensure that the directions/observations of the Hon'ble Court are followed.

(xi) CEIs which are in the process of conducting admission tests may decide on the cut-off marks for the OBC category well in time, so that consistent with the standards of education of the CEIs, sufficient number of eligible OBC candidates are available for selection on the basis of *inter-se* merit against the reserved seats.

(xii) CEIs which are yet to come out with application forms are expected to expeditiously insert the rule of exclusion/criteria of exclusion for the creamy layer, so that at the application stage itself the creamy layer could be identified, and only eligible candidates belonging to the OBC category are considered for the subsequent selection process and admissions against the reserved seats.

(xiii) Central Educational Institutions who are yet to advertise for the process of selection and admissions, shall ensure that the attention of candidates intending to apply against the reserved seats is as per the norms laid dawn.

While the above clarification is in respect of reservation in admission against the seats for the OBCs, CEIs are also to bear in mind that there may be a proportionate increase in the seats for the categories of SCs and STs also, while the extant procedure of selection or cut-off marks for these categories shall continue to be in force.

Institutions of Excellence in Respect of Which Office Memorandum is not Applicable

Sl. No.	*Names of the Institutions of Excellence, etc.*
1.	Homi Bhabha National Institute, Mumbai and its constituent units, namely:
	(i) Bhabha Atomic Research Centre, Trombay
	(ii) Indira Gandhi Centre for Atomic Research, Kalpakkam
	(iii) Raja Ramanna Centre for Advanced Technology, Indore
	(iv) Institute for Plasma Research, Gandhinagar
	(v) Variable Energy Cyclotron Centre, Kolkata
	(vi) Saha Institute of Nuclear Physics, Kolkata
	(vii) Institute of Physics, Bhubaneshwar
	(viii) Institute of Mathematical Sciences, Chennai
	(ix) Harish-Chandra Research Institute, Allahabad
	(x) Tata Memorial Centre, Mumbai

(*Contd.*)

Sl. No.	*Names of the Institutions of Excellence, etc.*
2.	Tata Institute of Fundamental Research, Mumbai
3.	North-Eastern Indira Gandhi Regional Institute of Health and Medical Science, Shillong
4.	National Brain Research Centre, Manesar, Gurgaon
5.	Jawaharlal Nehru Centre for Advanced Scientific Research, Bangalore
6.	Physical Research Laboratory, Ahmedabad
7.	Space Physics Laboratory, Thiruvananthapuram
8.	Indian Institute of Remote Sensing, Dehradun

7

Minority Education
Problems and Prospects

7.1 CONSTITUTIONAL PROVISIONS

Articles 29 and 30 provide for the 'Cultural and Educational Rights of the Minorities'.

Meaning of a Minority

The Constitution is silent on the meaning and definition of a minority. However, five religious communities, viz. Muslims, Christians, Sikhs, Buddhists and Zorastrians (Parsis) have been notified as minorities as per provisions under the National Commission for Minorities (NCM) Act, 1992. These five communities constitute about 18.47 per cent of the country's population.

7.2 CONSTITUTIONAL MEASURES

National Commission

The Government of India has set up the following Commissions for the welfare of the minorities:

1. National Commission for Minorities (1992)
2. National Commission for Religious and Linguistic Minorities (2005)

National Commission for Minorities: The National Commission for Minorities (NCM) was set up as a Statutory body in 1993 through the enactment of National Commission for Minorities Act, 1992. In November 2004, it was decided to amend the Constitution to grant constitutional status to the NCM. Accordingly, the Government introduced a Constitution (One hundred and Third Amendment) Bill, 2004 and National Commission for Minorities (Repeat) Bill, in the Lok Sabha on 23rd December, 2004. The National Commission for Minorities is responsible to safeguard the interests of minorities, which broadly relates to atrocities by the police, service matters, minority educational institutions and disputes relating to religious places. After taking cognisance of the complaints, reports are called for from the concerned authorities. On receipt of the reports, the Commission makes appropriate recommendations to the concerned authorities.

National Commission for Religious and Linguistic Minorities: The Government of India has been seized of the welfare needs of socially and economically backward sections among religious and linguistic minorities. For having a detailed examination to determine the criteria for identifications of socially and economically-backward sections among religious and linguistic minorities and to suggest measures for their welfare, the Government has constituted a National Commission for Religious and Linguistic Minorities with the following terms of reference:

(a) to suggest criteria for identification of socially and economically backward sections among religious and linguistic minorities;

(b) to recommend measures for welfare of socially and economically backward sections among religious and linguistic minorities, including reservation in education and government employment;

(c) to suggest the necessary constitutional, legal and administrative modalities, as required for the implementation of their recommendations; and to present a Report of their deliberations and recommendations.

The has Commission started functioning with effect from since 21 March, 2005.

Special Officer for Linguistic Minorities: The Office of the Special Officer for Linguistic Minorities (commonly known as the Commissioner for Linguistic Minorities) was created in July 1957, in pursuance of the provisions of Article 350-B of the Constitution. The Commissioner for Linguistic Minorities of India (CLM) has his Headquarters at Allahabad with Regional Offices at Kolkata, Belgaum and Chennai.

7.3 EDUCATIONAL DEVELOPMENT

Among the minorities, the Muslim community, being the largest minority community has received special attention.

Two important schemes, namely the scheme of Area Intensive Programme for Educationally Backward Minorities and the Scheme of Financial Assistance for the Modernisation of Madarsa Education had been in operation before the 10th Five Year Plan. In the 10th Five Year Plan, these schemes were merged. The merged scheme includes—

Madarsa Modernisation

Under this scheme component salary of 2 teachers per Madarsa @ Rs. 3,000 per month per teacher for teaching modern subjects like science, mathematics, English and social studies has been provided. In addition one time grant of Rs. the 7000 for the purchase of science/maths kits per Madarsa and another grant of Rs. 7,000 for book banks and strengthening of libraries are also given. The assistance is available to institutions all over the country.

The plan allocation for the 10th Five Year Plan for the scheme was Rs. 83.92 crore.

7.4 INSTRUCTIONAL DEVELOPMENT

Infrastructural Development

The objective of this component is to provide basic educational infrastructure in primary/upper primary and secondary schools where there is need for them and viability is established on the basis of a school mapping exercise. The target area identified is 325 blocks and 4 districts of Assam. This component is being implemented in this region only.

Since the beginning of the scheme the following physical targets have reportedly been achieved:

- opening/construction of buildings for 3010 primary/upper primary/secondary schools;
- establishment of 7 residential higher secondary schools for girls;
- construction of 3972 additional classrooms;
- upgradation of 79 primary schools to upper primary schools and high schools to higher secondary schools;
- construction of 31 hostel buildings for girls in higher secondary schools;
- toilets/urinals in 2540 schools;
- provision of teaching-learning material in 1303 primary/upper primary schools and library books, almirahs and furniture in 849 primary/upper primary/secondary schools;
- provision of drinking water in 113 primary/upper primary schools.
- electrification of 1230 primary/upper primary/secondary schools;
- provision of science rooms/laboratories in 102 primary/upper primary schools; and
- provision of 214 computers.

Educational Institutions

This Commission was set up through an ordinance on 11th November 2004 to advise the Central Government or any State Government on questions relating to education of minorities the to look into and complaints regarding violation of the constitutional protection guaranteed to minorities to establish and administer educational institutions of their choice and also to permit minority educational institutions to seek affiliation to scheduled central universities. Within one year of its establishment the Commission had received over 250 complaints/petitions and several suggestions for strengthening it.

7.5 EDUCATIONAL RIGHTS OF MINORITIES: SUPREME COURT JUDGEMENT (2002)*

Introduction

Article 29 and *Article 30* of the Constitution of India lay down certain safeguards/directions for the establishment and running of minority educational institutions. These articles are given below to have a background of the issue under reference.

Article 29. *Protection of Interests of Minorities*: (1) Any section of the citizens residing in the territory of India or any part thereof having a distinct language, script or culture of its own shall have the right to conserve the same.

(2) No citizen shall be denied admission into any educational institution maintained by the State or receiving aid out of State funds on grounds only of religion, race, caste, language or any of them.

Article 30. *Right of Minorities to Establish and Administer Educational Institutions*: (1) All minorities, whether based on religion or language, shall have the right to establish and administer educational institutions of their choice.

(1A) In making any law providing for the compulsory acquisition of any property of an educational institution established and administered by a minority, referred to in clause (1), the State shall ensure that the amount fixed by or determined under such law for the acquisition of such property is such as would not restrict or abrogate the right guaranteed under that clause.

(2) The state shall not, in granting aid to educational institutions, discriminate against any educational institution on the ground that it is under the management of a minority, whether based on religion or language.

From time-to-time several cases came up before the High Courts and the Supreme Court. The judgement given by a Constitutional Bench of the Supreme Court on October 31, 1992 is considered as a landmark judgement as regards the educational institutions run by the minorities. The Constitution Bench consisted of eleven judges. Main judgement was given by seven judges. Four judges gave different interpretations.

---

* P.D. Mathew S.J., '*The Landmark Judgement of the Supreme Court on Educational Rights of Minorities*', Indian Social Institute, New Delhi, 2002.

Highlights of the Judgement

- All citizens have right to establish and administer educational institutions.
- The right to administer minority educational institutions is not absolute.
- State can apply regulations to unaided MEIs (Minority Educational Institutions) to achieve educational excellence.
- Aided MEIs should admit certain percentage of non-minority students.
- Percentage of non-minority students to be admitted to an aided MEI is to be decided by the State or University.
- Fees to be charged by unaided MEI cannot be regulated but no institution can charge capitation fee.
- State can prescribe minimum qualifications for teachers and the principal in an unaided MEI.
- Tribunal headed by District Judge should be constituted for redressal of grievance of employees of MEI.
- State can provide the manner of admission in case of an aided MEI to ensure that it is done on the basis of merit.
- Merit could be determined through common entrance test.
- Unaided MEI could have their own procedure for admission but the same had to be fair and transparent.

7.6 THE NATIONAL COMMISSION FOR MINORITY EDUCATIONAL INSTITUTIONS ACT, 2004

Functions and Powers of the Commission

(a) To advise the Central Government or any State Government on any question relating to the education of minorities that may be referred to it.

(b) To grant minority status to any educational institution with prejudice to the provisions contained in the National Commission for Minorities Act, 1992.

(c) To enquire, *suo motu*, or on a petition presented to it by any Minority Educational Institution, or any person on its behalf into complaints regarding deprivation or violation of rights of minorities to establish and administer educational institutions of their choice and any dispute relating to the affiliation to a University and report its finding to the appropriate Government for its implementation;

(d) To intervene in any proceeding involving any deprivation or violation of the educational rights of the minorities before a court with the leave of such court;

(e) To review the safeguards provided by or under the Constitution, or any law for the time being in force, for the protection of educational rights of the minorities and recommend measures for their effective implementation;

(f) To specify measures to promote and preserve the minority status and character of institutions of their choice established by minorities;

(g) To decide all questions relating to the status of any institution as a Minority Educational Institution and declare its status as such;

(h) To make recommendations to the appropriate Government for the effective implementation of programmes and schemes relating to the Minority Educational Institutions; and

(i) To do such other acts and things as may be necessary, incidental or conducive to the attainment of all or any of the objects of the Commission.

Appeal Against the Order of the Commission

1. Any person aggrieved by the order of refusal to grant no objection certificate may prefer an appeal against such an order of the Commission.

2. An appeal under sub-section (1) shall be filed within thirty days from the date of the order referred to in sub-section (1) communicated to the applicant:

Provided that the Commission may entertain an appeal after the expiry of the said period of thirty days, if it is satisfied that there was sufficient cause for not filing it within that period.

3. An appeal to the Commission shall be made in such form as may be prescribed and shall be accompanied by a copy of the order against which the appeal has been filed.

4. The Commission, after hearing the parties, shall pass an order, as soon as may be practicable, and give such directions as may be necessary or expedient to give effect to its orders or to prevent abuse of its process or to secure the ends of justice.

5. An order made by the Commission under sub-section (4) shall be executable by the Commission as a decree of a civil court and the provisions of the Code of Civil Procedure, 1908 (5 of 1908), so far as may be, shall apply as they apply in respect of a decree of a civil court.

Power of Commission to investigate matters relating to deprivation of educational rights of minorities

(1) The Commission shall have the powers to investigate complaints relating to deprivation of the educational rights of minorities.

(2) The Commission may, for the purpose of conducting any investigation, pertaining to a complaint under this Act, utilise the services of any officer of the Central Government or any State Government with the

concurrence of the Central Government or the State Government, as the case may be.

7.7 PRIME MINISTER'S NEW 15-POINT PROGRAMME FOR THE WELFARE OF MINORITIES

The 15-point welfare programme for the minorities was announced by the Prime Minister and approved by the Cabinet in 2006. The programme has the following components:

1. Enhancing Opportunities for Education
2. Equitable Share in Economic Activities and Employment
3. Improving the Living Conditions of Minorities

Enhancing Opportunities for Education

(1) *Equitable Availability of ICDS Services*: The Integrated Child Development Services (ICDS) Scheme is aimed at holistic development of children and pregnant/lactating mothers from disadvantaged sections, by providing services through Anganwadi Centres such as supplementary nutrition, immunisation, health check-up, referral services, pre-school and non-formal education. A certain percentage of the ICDS projects and Anganwadi Centres were to be located in blocks/villages with a substantial population of minority communities to ensure that the benefits of this scheme are to be equitably available to such communities also.

(2) *Improving Access to School Education*: Under the Sarva Shiksha Abhiyan, the Kasturba Gandhi Balika Vidyalaya Scheme, and other similar Government schemes, it will be ensured that a certain percentage of such schools are located in villages/localities having a substantial population of minority communities.

(3) *Greater Resources for Teaching Urdu*: Central assistance will be provided for recruitment and posting of Urdu language teachers in primary and upper primary schools that serve a population in which at least one-fourth belong to that language group.

(4) *Modernising Madarsa Education*: The Central Plan Scheme of Area Intensive and Madarsa Modernisation Programme provides basic educational infrastructure in areas of concentration of educationally backward minorities and resources for the modernisation of Madarsa education. Keeping in view the importance of addressing this need, this programme was to be substantially strengthened and implemented effectively.

(5) *Scholarships for Meritorious Students from Minority Communities*: Schemes for pre-matric and post-matric scholarships for students from minority communities was to be formulated and implemented.

(6) *Improving Educational Infrastructure through the Maulana Azad Education Foundation*: The Government was to provide all possible

assistance to Maulana Azad Education Foundation (MAEF) to strengthen and enable it to expand its activities more effectively.

7.8 THE SACHAR COMMITTEE ON SOCIAL, ECONOMIC AND EDUCATIONAL STATUS OF THE MUSLIM COMMUNITY IN INDIA (2005-06)

Background of the Constitution of the Committee

For a long time it had been felt that there was a lack of authentic information about the social, economic and educational status of the Muslim Community of India which comes in the way of planning, formulating and implementing specific interventions, policies and programmes to address the issues relating to the socio-economic backwardness of this community. Therefore, the Government of India constituted a High Level Committee, to prepare a comprehensive report with in March 2005 covering these aspects. The Committee gave its report in 2006.

Major Observations and Recommendations: Extracts from the Report

The report probed the question of whether different socio-religious categories (SRCs) in India have had an equal chance to reap the benefits of development, with a focus on Muslims in India. Since the mandate of this Committee was primarily on equity, the Report essentially dealt with the relative deprivation of Muslims vis-à-vis other SRCs in various dimensions of development.

Analysis by the committee shows that while there is considerable variation in the conditions of Muslims across states (and among the Muslims, those who identified themselves as OBCs and others), the Community exhibits/deficits and deprivation in practically all dimensions of development. In fact, by and large, Muslims rank somewhat above SCs/STs but below Hindu-OBCs, Other Minorities and Hindu-General (mostly upper castes) in almost all indicators considered. Among the states that have large Muslim populations, the situation is particularly grave in the states of West Bengal, Bihar, Uttar Pradesh and Assam. Interestingly despite such deficits, the Community has lower infant mortality rates and sex-ratios. In addition to the 'development deficit', the perception among Muslims that they are discriminated against and excluded is widespread, which exacerbates the problem.

The Committee strongly suggested that the policies to deal with the relative deprivation of the Muslims in the country should sharply focus on inclusive development and 'mainstreaming' of the Community while respecting diversity. There is an urgent need to recognise diversity in residential, work and educational spaces, apart from enhancing inclusion of the really deprived SRCs in 'spaces' created by public programmes and policy interventions. The need for equity and inclusion in a pluralistic society can never be overemphasised. But the mechanisms to ensure equity and equality of opportunity to bring about inclusion should be such that diversity is achieved and at the same time the perception of discrimination is eliminated. This is only possible when the importance of Muslims as an intrinsic part of the diverse Indian social mosaic is squarely recognised.

General Policy Initiatives and Approaches

Need for Transparency, Monitoring and Data Availability

Availability of reliable data on a continuing basis on socio-economic is a prerequisite for good governance. Availability of such data would also make policy instruments like Right to Information Act more efficacious. The Committee had faced the acute problem of non-availability of reliable data and, therefore, had to launch an independent effort to collect, collate and, consolidate available data. The data obtained through these mechanisms with considerable difficulty was still not exhaustive enough to analyse several issues to committee's satisfaction. There is an immediate need, therefore, to make arrangements to collect data for different SRCs on a regular basis and make it available to researchers and the public.

The committee recommended a creation of a National Data Bank (NDB) where all relevant data for various SRCs were to be maintained. All the data was to be eventually computerised and made available on the Internet. There is an urgent need, therefore, to assess afresh the data needs for evaluating conditions of citizens by SRC status on a regular basis so as to understand and assess the flow of development benefits. The NDB should also be the repository of data on different beneficiary-oriented government programmes undertaken at the national and the state levels along with the details of beneficiaries drawn from different SRCs. Details of employment, credit flows, programme participation, etc. should also be shared by various national and state agencies and undertakings with the NDB from other agencies identified above as well as to obtain required information. It should be obligatory on the part of the relevant departments of the Central and State Governments to supply the information to the NDB.

Once such data are available there is a need to institutionalise the mechanisms for assessment and monitoring in order to suggest policy options on a timely basis. The Committee recommends the setting up of an autonomous Assessment and Monitoring Authority (AMA) to evaluate the extent of development benefits which accrue to different SRCs through various programmes.

Enhancing the Legal Basis for Providing Equal Opportunities

The widespread perception of discrimination among the Muslim community needs to be addressed. There are hardly any empirical studies that establish discrimination. Research in this area needs to be encouraged but is particularly difficult due to non-availability of data. Hopefully, better availability of data would result in more studies in this area. While equity in the implementation of programmes and better participation of the Community in the development process would gradually eliminate this perception of discrimination, there is a need to strengthen the legal provisions to eliminate such cases.

The Indian Constitution in 'Part III – Fundamental Rights' has exhaustively provided not only for equality of all citizens irrespective of their religion but has also provided special provisions for protecting the rights of minorities in respect of their religion, language and culture. Thus, any violation of the rights of the minority by the State could be challenged in a court of law. There are also institutions like National Human Rights Commission (NHRC), National Commission for Minorities (NCM) to look into complaints made by the minorities with respect to the State action. But, these mechanisms can only have a limited role and cannot look into many complaints arising on a day-to-day basis against non-State agencies. The minorities, many a time, may feel that there is discrimination against them in the matter of employment, housing, for obtaining loans from the public or private sector banks, or opportunities for good schooling. It is self-evident that if minorities have these perceptions, law must provide an effective mechanism which should examine their complaints and be able to give effective relief. It is imperative that if the minorities have certain perceptions of being aggrieved, all efforts should be made by the State to find a mechanism by which these complaints could be attended to expeditiously. This mechanism should operate in a manner which gives full satisfaction to the minorities that any denial of equal opportunities or bias or discrimination in dealing with them, either by public functionary or any private individual, will immediately be attended to and redress given.

It is a well-accepted maxim in law that not only must justice be done but it must appear to have been done. It is in that context that the Committee recommended that an Equal Opportunity Commission (EOC) should be constituted by the government to look into the grievances of deprived groups. An example of such a policy tool is the UK Race Relations Act, 1976.

Enhancing Participation in Governance

One reason for less than adequate participation in the development process may be due to inadequate participation in the governance structures. The Indian democracy provides opportunities for communities and groups of various social, economic and political orientations to democratically get elected and participate in different levels of 'governance' beginning from the grassroots to the state and national level political structures. Thus, democratic participation is possible for all communities within the country at a number of levels – national, the states/union territories and at the grassroots. The local self-governments – panchayats and zilla parishads in rural areas, and municipalities and corporations in urban areas — are crucial instruments in this context. Besides these institutions of parliamentary democracy, there are a number of para-governmental institutions which run on the principles of electoral democracy and public representation.

Over the last sixty years minorities have scarcely occupied adequate public spaces. The participation of Muslims in nearly all political spaces is low which can have an adverse impact on the Indian society and polity in the long run. The marginalised either have inadequate numbers that comes in the way of making their presence felt in the normal course of governance or they are not politically empowered. Given the power of numbers in a democratic polity, based on universal franchise, minorities in India lack effective agency and political importance. They do not have the necessary influence or the opportunity to either change or even influence events which enables their meaningful and active participation in development process. Therefore, there is a strong case to put mechanisms in place that enable them to engage in democratic processes at various levels of polity and governance. Mere material change will not bring about the true empowerment of the minorities; they need to acquire and be given the required collective agency.

Facilitate Creation of Common Public Spaces

Most poor children do not have access to parks, libraries and even study spaces within their own houses. Such spaces can enhance interaction among SRCs and also provide the much needed fillip to educational initiatives; such spaces can be used by the community or civil society to organise remedial classes, reading rooms and other constructive initiatives. The State should encourage such initiatives in mixed localities and across neighbourhoods so that children belonging to different SRCs can interact and at the same time pursue studies. These spaces can also be used for interaction and constructive activities among adults of different SRCs. Such initiatives are essentially a domain of civil society but mechanisms to encourage such activities through provision of unused/vacant municipal premises/land etc. can be quite useful.

Criticality of Education

Access to education is critical for benefiting from emerging opportunities that are accompanied by economic growth. The report brings out clearly the educational deprivation experienced by the Muslim community. From lower levels of enrolment to a sharp decline in participation in higher levels of education, the situation of Indian Muslims is indeed very depressing as compared to most other SRCs; in fact their situation seems to have worsened in relative terms. And the problem is more acute for girls/women. Reasons for this are varied – ranging from poverty to perceived discrimination resulting in alienating school environment. While the overall situation remains bad, the enrolment rates of Muslims have picked up in recent years and the policies should help sustain the momentum that can get created through this change. Our analysis also shows that the major problems lie in school education; the likelihood of Muslim children completing school education is significantly lower than other SRCs, except SCs/STs, once factors like household expenditure, place of residence, gender etc. are controlled for. Once the "hurdle" of school education is crossed, the differences across most SRCs in the likelihood of completing graduate studies narrow down and are at limes not very significant. Therefore, a sharper focus on school education is desirable.

Free and compulsory education up to the age of 14 is the responsibility of the State. And the fulfillment of this obligation is critical for the improvements in the educational conditions of Muslims, in fact, of all socio-economically deprived children. In addition, a sharper focus on a few areas listed below is desirable.

Adequate Reflection of Social Diversity in the Content of School Text Books

The school text book is one of the most enduring influences in the formative years of childhood. Along with the family, the school teaches the child not only the three Rs but values and attitudes that shape the child's character and create a sense of values. Given the influence of the text book, the Committee felt that it can work as an important instrument of imparting social values. The text book should not only reflect reality but also help in creating appropriate values. Since the children tend to read their text books several times, their familiarity with the text is significant and acts to reinforce the values being suggested in the text. If the texts do not reflect diversity or are derogatory with respect to specific communities, they can alienate children of those communities from the wider society. Simple things in the text books can sow the seeds for religious intolerance, create caste bias and/or reduce sensitivity to gender differences, while the intent and purpose of texts should be to do just the opposite. The Committee recommended that a process of evaluating the content of the school text books needed to be initiated to purge them of explicit and implicit content that may impart inappropriate social values, especially religious intolerance.

Initiatives in School Education

Muslims have the largest percentage share of children in the age group of less than 10 years with 27 per cent falling in this range as compared to the 23 per cent for the country as a whole. However, the current enrolment and continuation rates at elementary level (though picking up in recent years) are the lowest for the Muslims. These facts make primary education particularly important for the Community and the need to ensure that all children in the age group 0-14 have access to free and high quality education more urgent. In addition, the following initiatives are desirable:

- Given the fact that a substantial proportion of households in urban settlements live in one-room accommodations it is absolutely necessary to create local community study centres for students so that they can spend a few hours to concentrate on their studies. This is an area in which the government, NGOs and the corporate sector can cooperate.
- High quality Government schools should be set up in all areas of Muslim concentration.
- Exclusive schools for girls should be set up, particularly for the 9-12 standards. This would facilitate higher participation of Muslim girls in school education. In co-education schools more women teachers need to be appointed.
- Availability of primary education in one's mother tongue is constitutionally provided for. There is an urgent need to undertake appropriate mapping of Urdu speaking population and provide primary education in Urdu in areas where Urdu speaking population is concentrated.

Technical Education and Training for Non-matriculates

As noted in the chapter on education, majority of Muslim girls and boys fail in their matriculation examinations or drop-out before that. This group of children who have completed middle school but have not managed to study further needs to be incorporated in different types of technical training. The skill demands in the manufacturing and service sectors are changing continuously. And for many of these, highly educated/trained persons may not be required and youth with middle school education with adequate technical training may be appropriate for meeting these needs. However, almost all vocational training programmes run by the ITI's and polytechnics require a matriculation certificate. The Committee recommended that:

- The pre-entry qualification for admission to ITIs should be reduced to Class VIII. The scope of ITI courses should be expanded to focus on emerging market needs including those of the retail sector.

- Skill development initiatives of ITIs and polytechnics should focus on sectors which have high growth potential and in which the Muslim population is concentrated. These training initiatives should also focus on areas where the minority population concentrated.
- The eligibility for such programmes should also be extended to the Madarssa educated children, as they are ineligible to get trained under many current formal technical education streams.

Initiatives for Higher Education

Our analysis has shown that there is a high "deficit" as far as Muslim population in the higher education is concerned. And this "deficit" is higher than for all SRCs except SCs/STs. It has been already mentioned, that the best long-term measure to correct this deficit is to increase school completion rates among the Muslims. In the medium and short run, a two-pronged strategy can be employed:

Strategy No. 1: The University Grants Commission (UGC) should be encouraged to evolve a system where part of the allocation to colleges and universities is linked to the diversity in the student population. Even private colleges, including those run by the minorities and which have affiliation with universities or are recognised by state bodies can be provided additional funds if they have a diverse student population and charge reasonable fees. As mentioned earlier, an appropriate diversity index will need to be developed for such purposes. It is advisable that the UGC undertakes a proactive exercise to sensitise the educational institutions with respect to the need to reflect diversity on these campuses.

The Muslims of some states like Andhra Pradesh, Karnataka, Tamil Nadu have established a number of 'minority managed professional institutions' which have opened up avenues for higher education for Muslims and other minorities. They need to get encouragement as community initiatives but even these institutions need to have diverse populations. Government financial aid to these institutions can be linked to low tuition and other fees and partly to diversity of student population. These 'minority institutions' are typically inaccessible to the poor from these communities. Low fees combined with merit-*cum*-means scholarships (partly funded from the additional government grants) would enhance participation of poor among the minorities.

Strategy No. 2: To facilitate admissions to the 'most backward' amongst all the SRCs in the regular universities and autonomous colleges, alternate admission criteria need to be evolved. The following example provides a rating/grading system that can potentially be used.

This system should help the poor among all communities. As a complement to the first strategy, part of state funding can also be linked to the use of such criteria in admissions by the educational institutions.

Total Points	100
■ Assessment of Merit to the maximum of	60
■ Assessment of Backwardness to the maximum of	40
Backwardness to be defined as the sum of the following (Each with about one-third weight)	
(1) Household income (income criteria to be revised periodically)	13
(2) Backward district (list to be updated on annual basis)/residence in a notified urban slum	13
(3) Backward class (assessed based on a combination of family occupation and caste)	14

Provision of Hostels

Providing hostel facilities at reasonable costs for students from minorities must be taken up on a priority basis. While this is required for all minority students, such facilities for girls in cities of all sizes are particularly desirable. The availability of such hostels would ensure that many girls would continue schooling (beyond secondary/college education) as they would not have to commute on a daily basis to access educational institutions located at a distance from their place of residence. Hostels are equally important in the context of boys accessing college education. Ideally, the provision of such facilities should be made in partnership with the Community; the State can facilitate Community initiatives in this area through grants and other support. The taluka headquarters and educational centers would be the best locations for such facilities.

Teacher Training Programme

Teacher training should compulsorily include in its curriculum components which introduce the importance of diversity/plurality within the country and sensitise teachers towards the needs and aspirations of Muslims and other marginalised communities. The implementation of this should be monitored by the National Council of Teacher Education (NCTE). The other issue is that of dearth of Muslim school teachers, especially women. Given the current education levels, the possibility of more Muslims opting for B.Ed course is limited. But more Muslims may be able to participate as para teachers. An effort should be made to enhance participation of Muslims in this cadre as an interim measure.

There are only a few teachers who can teach in the Urdu medium. Given the commitment to provide primary education in the child's mother tongue, the State is required to run Urdu medium schools. This in turn would require teachers capable of teaching in the Urdu medium. Preference to teachers who can instruct through Urdu medium is desirable in all teacher training departments in states where Urdu speaking population is substantial.

Interventions to Support the Urdu Language

While Urdu language is not a language of the Muslims alone, contemporary circumstances make it appear to be so. The language has been neglected. The fallout of this has been inadequate access to education in the mother tongue for many Urdu speaking children. The neglect has also resulted in poor performance of Urdu medium school students because of poor infrastructural facilities and absence of adequate number of qualified teachers. It is imperative that Urdu language is supported to provide a regular stream of Urdu teachers. Moreover, for secondary education the distortions made in the Three Language Formula should be corrected in order to accommodate Urdu in schools of the Hindi region. In addition, three more measures are desirable:

- Often Urdu schools have teachers who have no knowledge of Urdu. This problem is partly compounded by the fact that posts of Urdu teachers are reserved for the SCs/STs and such candidates are not available. This anomaly needs to be corrected urgently.
- High quality Urdu medium schools can be opened in those parts of the country wherever there is demand for them. However, it needs to be ensured that good quality text books are available in Urdu language and the products of these schools are employable.
- Urdu should be introduced as an optional subject in all government and government-aided schools in states having a substantial Urdu speaking population.

Madarssas and Mainstream Education

Madarssas have played an important role in providing religious education to the Muslim population. They also provide 'mainstream' education in many cases and several of them are in the process of modernising their curriculum. While this is an important initiative of the community to improve educational conditions, it is important to take note of the fact that less than 4 per cent of the Muslim children in the school going age actually attend the full time regular Madarssas. Therefore, the modernised Madarssas are unlikely to satisfy the educational demand of the Community and the State will have to make provision for mainstream schools in areas where such schools are not available. In other words,

Madarssas should not be looked upon as alternatives to the regular school, but a complement. The following steps seem desirable:

- Work out mechanisms whereby Madarssas can be linked with a higher secondary school board so that students wanting to shift to a regular/mainstream education can do so after having passed from a Madarssa.
- Provision of "equivalence" to Madarssa certificates/degrees for subsequent admissions into institutions of higher level of education. Flexibility should be introduced so as to enable Madarssa graduates to move across to regular mainstream education after graduating from these institutions, if they so wish. In other words the opportunity should be made available to them, especially in courses where admission is done through an entrance test/competitive examination.

Enhancing Access to Credit and Government Programmes

Lack of access to credit is a more serious problem for the Community as a significantly larger proportion of workers are engaged in self-employment, especially home-based work. Therefore, non-availability of credit can have far-reaching implications for the socio-economic and educational status of the Community. Wherever comparative analysis between Muslims and other minorities has been carried out it has been shown that the access of other minorities to credit from banks and other programmes is far better than Muslims.

The Committee, therefore, recommended promoting and enhancing access to Muslims in Priority Sector Advances.

The detailed analysis of Muslim participation in government employment and other programmes has shown very limited participation in both. While no discrimination is being alleged, it may be desirable to have experts drawn from the Community on relevant interview panels and Boards. This practice is already in vogue in the case of SCs/STs.

The review of Government programmes suggests that Muslims have not benefited much from them. At times the Muslims do not have adequate participation as beneficiaries; when participation is adequate, the total amounts allocated to the programme are too low to make any meaningful impact. The current formats in which the data are kept do not permit easy assessment of the benefits that have accrued to various SRCs. Detailed data should be collected regularly on the participation of different SRCs in government programmes, both at the State and the Central level. As suggested earlier such data should be made available to the NDB which will maintain it and make it available to users.

Last but not the least, although there are many Centrally Sponsored Schemes (CSS) and Central Plan Schemes (CPS) available for the welfare of SCs, STs and OBCs, such schemes for the welfare of minorities are rare.

Even the available schemes are inadequately funded. Overall, targeting backward districts and clusters where special artisanal groups exist, will ensure a sharp reduction in disparities of access and attainment. The Central Government should introduce a few schemes with large outlays for welfare of minorities with an equitable provision for Muslims.

Improving Employment Opportunities and Conditions

The country is going through a high growth phase. This is the time to help the underprivileged to utilise new opportunities through skill development and education. A large segment of the Muslim community is engaged in self-employment activities. Besides, a significant proportion, especially women, is actually engaged in home-based work. While some of these workers are engaged in sectors that have experienced growth, many are engaged in occupations/sectors that are stagnant.

Given these conditions, the following initiatives seem desirable:

- Provide financial and other support to initiatives built around occupations where Muslims are concentrated and that have growth potential. These initiatives can take the form of interventions where existing skills of the workers are combined with knowledge of modern management practices, new technology, and emerging market needs.
- Since skill upgradation needs might be high in such clusters, location of ITIs, polytechnics and other institutions that provide skill training to non-matriculates need to be located here. Availability of such institutions in the vicinity would not only help those sections of the workers who are involved in growth-oriented industries but also those who wish to move to new sectors through skill formation or upgradation.
- Given the precarious conditions of the self-employed persons in the informal sector, especially the home-based workers, it is desirable to have a mandated social security system for such workers. Casual workers in the informal sector should also be able to participate in such schemes.
- A more transparent recruitment system will help to build public confidence in the system. It is not being suggested that inclusion of minorities in selection committees will improve the chances that Muslims will get selected, it can surely improve the confidence of Muslim applicants during the selection process.
- It is imperative to increase the employment share of Muslims particularly in contexts where there is a great deal of public dealing. Their public visibility will endow the larger Muslim community with a sense of confidence and involvement and help them in accessing these facilities in larger numbers and greater

proportion. To achieve this, efforts should be made to increase the employment share of Muslims amongst the teaching community health workers, police personnel, bank employees and so on. Employers should be encouraged to endorse their organisations as 'Equal Opportunity Institutions' so that applicants from all SRCs may apply. A time bound effort in this direction is desirable.

Enhancing the Efficacy of Infrastructure Provision

Inadequate availability of infrastructure is one of the many problems that Muslims share with all poor especially the disadvantaged SRCs in the country. While the number of service providers from the non-governmental organisations is on the rise, public provision of infrastructure remains critical and desirable. Sensitivity to the issues of different SRCs is very important to the delivery of services such as primary education, health, etc.

Encouraging Community Initiatives

Many of the measures suggested above would become more efficacious if there is community participation. In fact, partnerships between the government, the community and the private sector may be quite useful to deal with problems faced by the Muslims. In this context, better utilisation of Wakf properties can provide partnership opportunities.

7.9 SUMMARY OF OBSERVATIONS AND RECOMMENDATIONS

1. Education

(a) *Present State of Excess*

Access to education is critical to benefiting from emerging opportunities that go with economic growth. The right to education is a fundamental right; the Report established the extent of educational deprivation experienced by the Muslim community. Muslims are at a double disadvantage with low levels of education combined with low quality education. Their deprivation increases many-folds as the level of education rises. 25 per cent of Muslim children in the 6-14 year age group have either never attended school or have dropped out. At the level of higher education, less than 4 per cent Muslims are graduates or diploma holders as against the national average of 7 per cent for the age group 20 and above. At the post-graduate level, only one out of twenty students is a Muslim.

(b) *Recommendations*

(i) Regular affordable school education that is available to any other child in India should be made available to Muslims in all localities.

(ii) Primary education in mother tongue is equally important.

(iii) Access to government schools for Muslim children is limited. This is particularly so in regard to girls for whom the non-availability of schools within easy reach hampers access to education at the primary level.

More schools for girls should be set up in localities of Muslim concentration, particularly for the 9-12 standards. This would facilitate higher participation of girls in school education. Induction of more female teachers, provision of hostels for girls and transport facilities would be helpful.

(iv) Institution of more scholarships for professional and technical courses would encourage students to avail greater measure of opportunities in higher education.

(v) Skill development initiatives for those who have not completed school education may also be particularly relevant for some section of Muslims given the occupational structure. The pre-entry qualifications for admission to ITI courses should be reduced to Class VIII. The scope of ITI courses should be expanded to focus on emerging market needs. The eligibility of such programmes should also be extended to Madarssa educated children.

2. Economy and Employment Opportunities

(a) *Present Status*

The participation of Muslims in regular salaried jobs, especially in the government or large public and private sector enterprises, is much less than workers of other SRCs (Socio-religious Communities). Instead, Muslims have higher than average reliance on self-employment, home-based work and are concentrated in self-employed manufacturing and trade activities. Given the informal nature of their work participation, they tend to be more vulnerable than other workers with regard to work related industries in terms of type of contract, availability of social benefits and method of payment.

Since a large section of the Muslim workers are engaged in self-employment, improvements in employment opportunities for them requires a sharpen focus on skill development and related matters.

(b) *Recommendations*

(i) Specific programmes for self-employed or home-based workers to provide skill, credit, technology and market support in backward districts are needed. These programmes should effectively combine modern managerial, technical and design skills with artisanal skills to create effective intervention strategies.

(ii) ITIs, polytechnics and other institutions, that provide skill training to non-matriculates, need to be located in backward and minority concentration districts.

(iii) Alternative mechanisms, including but not confined to micro financing bodies, should be identified and charged with the task of providing institutional support like market linkages, skill upgradation and funding of trades being run by the Muslims artisans.

(iv) The Small Industrial Development Bank of India (SIDBI) should set aside a dedicated fund for training for minorities under its Entrepreneurial Development Programme.

(v) Imparting skills both to those who have completed school education, and those who have dropped out of school but have completed middle education, needs to be reassessed. Most existing technical training programmes require higher secondary education. Given the school completion rates of Muslims and the significant need for skill upgradation, provision of certain types of skill training after middle education may be useful.

(vi) Given the precarious conditions of self-employed persons in the informal sector, especially the home-based workers, it is desirable to have a mandated social security system for such workers. Since the government is already in the process of drafting a scheme to cover the unorganised workers, an early implementation would benefit a large section of the Muslim population along with helping the larger segment of the informal sector workforce.

3. Access to Bank Credit

(a) *Present Status*

The access of Muslims to bank credit, including the Priority Sector Advance (PSA), is limited and this is well-documented. The average size of credit is also meagre compared with other groups both in public and private sector banks. The percentage of households availing banking facilities is much lower in villages where the share of Muslim population is high. While part of this could be due to lower demand for credit owing to low income levels of the community, another reason for such an outcome could be non-availability of banking facilities in these villages.

This is a serious problem as a significantly larger proportion of Muslims are engaged in self-employment, especially home-based work. Non-availability of credit can have far-reaching implications for the socio-economic and educational status of Muslims.

(b) *Recommendations*

(i) Non-availability of banking facilities should be addressed on a priority basis by providing incentives to banks to open more branches in backward districts.

(ii) To empower Muslims economically, it is necessary to ensure smooth flow of credit/micro-credit and Priority Sector Advances. Steps should be taken to specifically direct credit, create awareness of various credit schemes, organise entrepreneurial development programmes, and bring transparency in reporting of information about provision of banking services.

(iii) A policy to enhance the participation of minorities in the micro-credit schemes of NABARD should be laid down. This should spell out the intervention required by NABARD and could be a mix of target and incentive schemes to enhance the participation of Muslims in micro-credit.

(iv) The practice of identifying 'negative geographical zones' where bank credit and other facilities are not easily provided needs to be reviewed to enable people to benefit fully from banking facilities in the light of government's socio-economic objectives of inclusion.

4. Access to Social and Physical Infrastructure and Government Programmes

(a) *Present Status*

Muslims are concentrated in locations with poor infrastructural facilities. This affects their access to basic services like education, health facilities, transport etc.

Although there are many Centrally Sponsored Schemes and Central Plan Schemes available for the welfare of SCs, STs and OBCs, such schemes for the welfare of minorities are very few, are inadequately funded and have not benefited many Muslims.

(b) *Recommendations*

(i) Public investment in infrastructure in Muslim concentration areas is urgently required to promote socio-economic development and access to public services.

(ii) A focus on backward districts and clusters where special artisanal groups exist will ensure a sharp reduction in disparities of access and attainment.

(iii) Central Government should introduce a few schemes with large outlays for welfare of minorities with an equitable provision for Muslims.

(iv) A periodic monitoring and assessment of welfare and development programmes, and the extent to which the benefits accrue to Muslims, is imperative. The monitoring mechanism should be multi-level and should have a civil society component. This would enhance public confidence.

5. Public Employment and Recruitment Procedures

(a) *Present Status*

Analysis of data has shown very limited Muslim participation in government employment and other programmes. Lack of access to regular salaried jobs, especially in the public sector, has been a matter of major concern. The deficit in regular employment, especially in salaried jobs in the public sector or the much larger private sector, needs to be corrected.

(b) *Recommendations*

(i) It is imperative to increase the public employment share of Muslims particularly in areas requiring a good deal of public dealing. To achieve this, efforts should be made to increase the employment share of Muslims in the teaching community, health workers, police personnel, bank employees and other similar callings.

(ii) It would be desirable to have experts drawn from the Muslim community on relevant interview panels and Boards. This practice is already in vogue in the case of SCs/STs.

(iii) Measures like undertaking a visible recruitment process in areas and districts with high percentage of Muslims, job advertisements in Urdu and vernacular newspapers and other media, or simple messages like 'women, minority, and backward class candidates are encouraged to apply', should be undertaken to promote participation in public employment.

7.10 STATUS OF IMPLEMENTATION OF THE FOLLOW-UP ACTION ON THE RECOMMENDATIONS OF THE SACHAR COMMITTEE

I. *Special Development Initiatives*

- Multi-sectoral Development Programme for minority concentration districts (MCDs)
    - Identified 90 minority concentration districts (MCDs) which are backward in basic amenities and socio-economic parameters.
    - Baseline survey carried out to identify 'development deficits'. Thirteen reports already received.
    - Multi-sectoral development programme approved for addressing the 'development deficits' in areas of education, sanitation, pucca housing, drinking water and electricity supply etc.
- Special Development Initiatives in Urban Areas
    - Recommendations of an inter-ministerial task force set up to consider improvement in civic amenities and economic opportunities in 338 class I & II towns, with substantial minority population.

II. *Measures to Improve Access to Credit*

- All public sector banks directed to open more branches in identified minority concentration districts. 496 branches opened in 2007-08.
- Reserve Bank of India (RBI) revised the Master Circular on priority sector lending on 5.7.2007. Public sector banks were asked to step up lending to minorities from 9 per cent to 15 per cent over the next three years.
- Revised master circular provides for setting up of a special cell to ensure smooth flow of credit to minorities.

III. *Measures to Improve Access to Education*

- Under SSA, States advised to give primacy to opening Girls in only Upper Primary Schools in minority concentration areas. 270 KGBVs sanctioned in blocks having more than 20 per cent population of Muslims.
- Priority to be given to opening of secondary/senior secondary schools in areas of Muslim concentration. A scheme for universalising secondary education was being formulated.
- New Jan Shikshan Sansthans would be set up in all districts, with a substantial population of Muslims, not covered as yet with such Sansthans. Three JSSs sanctioned in minority concentration areas.
- Mid-day meal programme extended to upper primary level in all 3479 educationally backward blocks.
- Seventy seven blocks, with a high concentration of Muslims identified for establishment of BITEs for teacher education. Scheme for selling up of BITEs being modified.
- Provision of more girl's hostels in colleges and universities in minority concentration districts proposed under the existing University Grants Commission (UGC) scheme. Proposed also to open new polytechnics with hostel facilities in MCDs.
- The Madarssa modernisation programme being revised to make it more attractive by providing better salary to teachers, increased assistance for books, teaching aids, and computers, introduce vocational subjects, etc.
- UGC asked to work out modalities so that universities are encouraged to recognise Madarssa qualifications.
- NCERT has prepared text books for all classes in the light of the NCF 2005, except class V and VIII.
- Requirement of Urdu teachers from the states was being ascertained and sanctioned for Andhra Pradesh and Himachal Pradesh.

VI. *Plan for Skill Development*

- Inter-ministerial group for skill and entrepreneurial

development constituted for preparation of a comprehensive plan for development of artisanal clusters.

VII. *Initiatives for Affirmative Action and Social Inclusion*

- Affirmative Action
- Expert group constituted to study and recommend the structure and functions of an Equal Opportunity Commission.
- Expert group constituted for evolving an appropriate Diversity Index to measure diversity in the areas of education, housing, and employment.
- A National Data Bank, to compile data on the various socio-economic and basic amenities parameters for socio-economic religious communities, set up in the Ministry of Statistics and Programme Implementation.
- An autonomous Assessment & Monitoring Authority (AMA), to analyse data collected for taking appropriate and corrective policy decisions, set up in the Planning Commission.
- Unorganised Sector Social Security Bill, to provide safeguards to workers in the unorganised sector, a large proportion of them being from the minority communities, introduced in Rajya Sabha.
- Concerns raised by the Sachar Committee on the delimitation of constituencies considered by a High Level Committee.
- *Social Inclusion*
    - Thirteen Universities provided Rs. 40 lakhs each for starting centres for studying social exclusion and inclusive policy for minorities and SCs and STs.
    - Instructions issued to training institutes to include in their induction and in-training courses a module on social inclusion to sensitise government employees.

7.11 FOLLOW UP ACTION ON SACHAR COMMITTEE REPORT

The Government of India appointed a Committee to suggest a follow up programme on the recommendations of the Sachar Committee. The Cabinet in May 2007, approved the following measures for providing education of the Minorities:

- To provide merit-cum means scholarships for 20,000 students pursuing technical and professional education.
- To give two pre and post-metric scholarships.
- To revise coaching scheme to improve employability and academic performance.
- To expand outreach of upper primary schools.

- To launch special literacy drive in districts with substantial minority population.
- To train more teachers.
- To increase allocation for opening women's hostels in schools and universities.
- To revise/modernise **'Madarsa'** programmes.
- To extend mid-day meal scheme.

8

Environment, Human Rights, Values and Women Education and Constitution

8.1 CONSTITUTION AND EDUCATION FOR ENVIRONMENT

Constitutional Provisions

The original Constitution of India did not include environment in the Directive Principles of State Policy. It was also not mentioned in any of the three lists of subjects, i.e. the Central List, State List and the Concurrent List.

The Constitution (Forty-Second Amendment) Act 1976 led to the insertion of Article 48A "Protection and Improvement of Environment and Safeguarding of Forests and Wild Life". The State shall endeavour "to protect and improve the environment and to safeguard the forests and wildlife of the country".

Apart from this, a new provision in the form of "Fundamental Duties" as Article 51A was also incorporated by the 42nd Constitutional Amendment, sub-clause (g) which states, "It shall be the duty of every citizen of India to protect and improve the natural environment including forests, lakes, rivers and wildlife and to have compassion for living creatures".

Implementation of policies and programmes relating to conservation of the country's natural resources, including lakes and rivers, its bio-diversity, forests and wildlife, ensuring the welfare of its animals and prevention and abatement of pollution are primary concerns of the Ministry of Environment and Forests under the Government structure. While implementing these policies and programmes, the Ministry is guided by the principle of sustainable development and enhancement of human well-being. The Ministry also serves as the nodal agency in the country for the United Nations Environment Programme (UNEP), South Asia Cooperative Environment Programme (SACEP), International Centre for Integrated Mountain Development (ICIMOD) and for the follow-up of the United Nation's Conference on Environment and Development (UNCED). The Ministry is also responsible for dealing with issues relating to multilateral bodies such as the Commission on Sustainable Development (CSD), Global

Environment Facility (GEF) and of regional bodies like Economic and Social Council for Asia and Pacific (ESCAP) and South Asian Association for Regional Cooperation (SAARC) on matters pertaining to environment.

The broad objectives of the Ministry are conservation and survey of flora, fauna, forests and wildlife, prevention and control of pollution, growth in forest cover by afforestation and regeneration of degraded areas, protection of environment and ensuring the welfare of animals. These objectives are well-supported by a set of legislative and regulatory measures, aimed at preservation, conservation and protection of the environment. Besides the legislative measures, a National Conservation Strategy and Policy Statement of Environment & Development, 1992, National Forest Policy, 1988, a Policy Statement on Abatement of Pollution 1992 and a National Environment Policy 2006 have also been evolved for guiding actions in future.

Environmental Education — The Newly Created Field

The conclusions and reports of UNESCO conferences and meetings such as the Belgrade Workshop (1975), the regional meetings held in 1976–1977 in Africa, the Arab States, Asia, Europe and Latin America, as well as several sub-regional meetings and workshops and the Tbilisi Conference (1977) have helped considerably in clarifying environmental education concepts and in formulating recommendations and proposals for future action.

By its very nature and function, environmental education forms an integral part of society.

Environmental education is a fundamental process through which persons at all possible educational levels (present and future citizens) become aware of, and concerned with, the environmental and its related problems, and acquire the knowledge, skills and determination needed to solve those problems. It is based on eco-development, i.e. scheme of action which is linked with undertakings in virtually every field and which could very well constitute a means of initiating and consolidating a new orientation for human development. In this sense, environmental education is a vast and multi-interdisciplinary pedagogical approach which involves all kinds of institutions and individuals. It is a process which enables us to acquire an understanding of the complex nature of the environment of which we are a part, and to appreciate humanity's dependence on, and responsibility for the environment. It is a means of achieving the goals of environmental management. It is a new educational approach to the relations of people and their environment. It is an experience based education which uses the totality of physical, natural and human resources of a milieu of a learning laboratory.

Aims

1. To develop constructive attitudes toward the environment, in both the philosophical and programmatical senses, which have not yet become an ingredient in everybody's thinking and acting. (*Final Report: Inter-Governmental Conference of Experts on the Scientific Bases for the Rational Use and Conservation of the Resources of the Biosphere, 1968*).

2. To develop awareness of and concern about the environment and its associated problems, and to develop knowledge, skills, attitudes, motivations and commitment to work individually and collectively towards solutions of current problems and prevention of new ones (APP. Fensham "*A Report on the Belgrade Conference on Environmental Education, Canberra, 1976*, p. 25).

3. To succeed in making individuals and communities understand the complex nature of the natural and the built environments resulting from the interaction of their biological, physical, social, economic and cultural aspects, and acquire the knowledge, values, attitudes, and practical skills to participate in a responsible and effective way in anticipating and solving environmental problems, and the management of the quality of the environment. (*Final Report of Tbilisi Inter-Governmental Conference on Environmental Education, 1977*).

National Policy on Education—NPE (1986 and as Amended in 1992) on Environment

In Part VIII entitled 'Reorienting the Content and Process of Education', the NPE under the caption 'Education and Environment', in Para 8.15 states, "There is a paramount need to create a consciousness of the environment. It must permeate all ages and all sections of society, beginning with the child. Environmental consciousness should inform teaching in schools and colleges. This aspect will be integrated in the entire educational process".

Introduction of Environment as a Compulsory Subject:

Supreme Court Judgement

On a public litigation petition, in 1991, the Supreme Court of India asked the NCERT and other concerned authorities to take steps to enforce compulsory education on environment in a graded way from the academic Session 1992–93. Since the order was not implemented even after eleven years, advocate M.C. Mehta filed an application to ensure implementation of the earlier order. The Supreme Court passed the order on April 22, 2004 for compliance.

The Supreme Court issued a notice on July 13, 2004 to the concerned authorities to inform it whether they had implemented orders for inclusion of environment as a subject in the institutions under their court.

It may be recalled that on April 22, 2004, the Court had endorsed a model syllabus prepared by the National Council of Educational Research and Training (NCERT) for introducing environmental studies as a compulsory subject from class one to class twelve.

The NCERT asked to be a model agency to monitor the implementation of the model syllabus in schools. The syllabus has been prepared after consultation with several experts and institutions, State Governments, the Central Pollution Control Board and Non-Government Organisations.

Environment (Protection) Act, 1986

General Powers of The Central Government

Power of Central Government to Take Measures to Protect and Improve Environment

(1) Subject to the provisions of this Act, the Central Government, shall have the power to take all such measures as it deems necessary or expedient for the purpose of protecting and improving the quality of the environment and preventing controlling and abating environmental pollution.

(2) In particular, and without prejudice to the generality of the provisions of sub-section (1), such measures may include measures with respect to all or any of the following matters, namely:

(i) coordination of actions by the State Governments, officers and other authorities—

(a) under this Act, or the rules made thereunder, or

(b) under any other law for the time being in force which is relatable to the objects of this Act;

(ii) planning and execution of a nation wide programme for the prevention, control and abatement of environmental pollution;

(iii) laying down standards for the quality of environment in its various aspects;

(iv) laying down standards for emission or discharge of environmental pollutants from various sources whatsoever:

Provided that different standards for emission or discharge may be laid down under this clause from different sources having regard to the quality or composition of the emission or discharge of environmental pollutants from such sources;

(v) restriction of areas in which any industries, operations or processes or class of industries, operations or processes shall not be carried out or shall be carried out subject to certain safeguards;

(vi) laying down procedures and safeguards for the prevention of accidents which may cause environmental pollution and remedial measures for such accidents;

(vii) laying down procedures and safeguards for the handling of hazardous substances;

(viii) examination of such manufacturing processes, materials and substances as are likely to cause environmental pollution;

(ix) carrying out and sponsoring investigations and research relating to problems of environmental pollution;

(x) inspection of any premises, plant, equipment, machinery, manufacturing or other processes, materials or substances and giving, by order, of such directions to such authorities, officers or persons as it may consider necessary to take steps for the prevention, control and abatement of environmental pollution;

(xi) establishment or recognition of environmental laboratories and institutes to carry out the functions entrusted to such environmental laboratories and institutes under this Act;

(xii) collection and dissemination of information in respect of matters relating to environmental pollution;

(xiii) preparation of manuals, codes or guides relating to the prevention, control and abatement of environmental pollution;

(xiv) such other matters as the Central Government deems necessary or expedient for the purpose of securing the effective implementation of the provisions of this Act.

(3) The Central Government may, if it considers it necessary or expedient so to do for the purpose of this Act, by order, published in the Official Gazette, constitute an authority or authorities by such name or names as may be specified in the order for the purpose of exercising and performing such of the powers and functions (including the power to issue directions under section 5) of the Central Government under this Act and for taking measures with respect to such of the matters referred to in sub-section (2) as may be mentioned in the order and subject to the supervision and control of the Central Government and the provisions of such order, such authority or authorities may exercise and powers or perform the functions or take the measures so mentioned in the order as if such authority or authorities had been empowered by this Act to exercise those powers or perform those functions or take such measures.

8.2 CONSTITUTION AND HUMAN RIGHTS EDUCATION

Human Rights, as commonly understood are the rights that every human being is entitled to enjoy irrespective of religion, race, caste, sex and nationality etc. These are moral claims which have been given the shape of legal rights. Because of being a human being, these rights are inherent.

After the Second World War, the desire of the nations to make the world free from future wars and ushering in an era of international peace led to the establishment of the United Nations Organisation (UNO) in 1945. The Charter contained a number of articles related to Human Rights.

The General Assembly of the UN passed the Universal Declaration of Human Rights on December 10, 1948.

The declaration includes Preamble and 32 Articles.

Broad Classification of Human Rights

- Civil
- Cultural
- Economic
- Educational
- Legal
- Political
- Social
- International

Civil Rights

Article 1: Dignity of all human beings
Article 2: Equality without any distinction
Article 3: Right to life, liberty and security
Article 4: Prohibition of slavery
Article 5: No inhuman treatment
Article 9: No arbitrary arrest
Article 12: Right to privacy
Article 13: Freedom of movement
Article 15: Right to nationality
Article 16: Right to marriage
Article 17: Right to own property

Cultural Rights

Article 24: Right to rest and leisure
Article 27: Right to participate in the cultural life of the community

Economic Rights

Article 23: Right to work
Article 25: Right to standard of living

Educational Rights

Article 26: Right to education

Legal Rights

Article 6, 7, 8, 10, 11: Right before law

Political Rights

Article 18: Freedom of thought etc.
Article 19: Freedom of expression
Article 20: Freedom of peaceful assembly

Article 21: Right to take part in the government
Article 30: Enjoyment of all rights

Social Rights

Article 22: Right to social security
Article 29: Duties to the community

International Rights

Article 14: Right to seek asylum in other countries
Article 28: Right to social and international order

All religions preach equality, love and affection towards others.

The successful working of democracy depends on the equality of opportunity to citizens.

The Constitution of India incorporates the fundamental values as contained in the UN Declaration of Human Rights. There are several Articles in Part III of the Constitution entitled 'Fundamental Rights' which are quite parallel to the Declaration. Likewise Part IV 'Directive Principles of State Policy' contains several provisions similar to human rights.

Article 14 of the Constitution provides: 'The State shall not deny to any person equality before law". This provision reflects the spirit of Article 2 of the UN Declaration of Human Rights. Article 19 of our Constitution gives every Indian the right to move freely, settle and reside in any part of India. This is commensurate with the Article 13 of the Declaration which provides for freedom of movement and residence.

Other provisions in our Constitution which are parallel to the Declaration of Human Rights include Right of Freedom of Worship and Propagation of Religion (Article 25), Right of Conservation of One's Language and Culture (Article 29); Right of Equal Pay for Equal Work for both Men and Women (Article 39) and Right to have Free and Compulsory Education up to the age of 14 (Article 21A).

Fundamental Rights in the Indian Constitution, Parallel to UN Declaration of Human Rights

	UN Declaration of Human Rights	*Indian Constitution and Fundamental Rights*
Article 1	Right to freedom	Article 19
Article 2	Freedom from discrimination	Article 15
Article 3	Right to life, liberty and security of persons	Article 21
Article 5	Freedom from torture or degrading treatment	Article 23
Article 6, 7	Equality before law	Article 14

	UN Declaration of Human Rights	*Indian Constitution and Fundamental Rights*
Article 8	Right to remedy through a competent tribunal	Article 32
Article 9	Freedom from arbitrary arrest	Article 22
Article 13	Right to freedom of movement and residence	Article 19 (d and e)
Article 18	Freedom of belief and religion	Article 25
Article 19	Freedom of opinion and information	Article 19 (a)
Article 20	Right to peaceful assembly and association	Article 19 (b)
Article 26	Right to education	Article 21 (a)
Article 30	Freedom from State or other interference in any of the above rights	Article 32

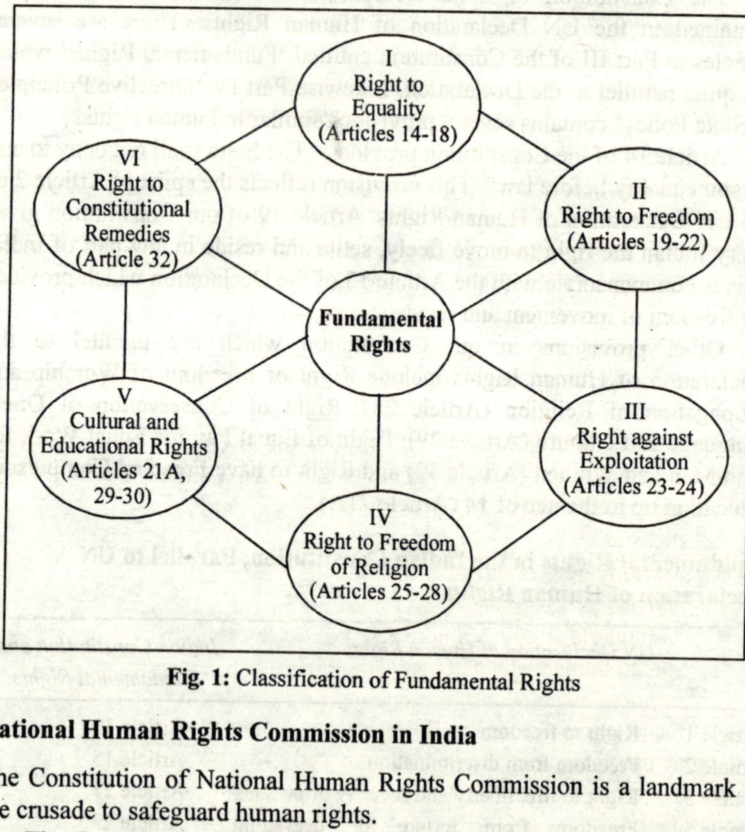

Fig. 1: Classification of Fundamental Rights

National Human Rights Commission in India

The Constitution of National Human Rights Commission is a landmark in the crusade to safeguard human rights.

The Commission started functioning on November 1, 1993. The eight members of the commission were to be as under:

1. Chairperson, a former Chief Justice of India.

2. A present or former Judge of the Supreme Court.
3. A present or former Chief Justice of a High Court.
4. and 5. Two members from amongst persons knowledgeable in the area of human rights.
6. Chairperson of the National Commission for Women.
7. Chairperson of the National Commission for SCs and STs.
8. Chairperson of the National Commission for Minorities.

Powers and Functions

NHRC can inquire on its own or on a petition presented to it by a victim or any person on his behalf into complaints of:

(i) Violation or abetment of violation of human rights.
(ii) Negligence in the prevention of such a violation by a public servant.

To perform its functions, the NHRC has been given following authorities:

- To intervene in any proceeding involving any allegation of violation of Human Rights pending before a court with the approval of such court.
- To visit, under intimation to a State government, any jail or any other institution under the control of the State government concerned, where persons are detained or lodged for purposes of treatment, reformation or protection, to study the living conditions of the inmates and make recommendations thereon.
- To review the safeguards provided by or under the Constitution or any law for the time being in force for the protection of Human Rights and recommend measures for their effective implementation.
- To review the factors, including acts of terrorism that inhibit the enjoyment of Human Rights and recommend appropriate remedial measures.
- To study treaties and other international instruments on Human Rights and make recommendations for their effective implementation.
- To undertake and promote research in the field of Human Rights; spread human rights literacy among various sections of society and promote awareness of the safeguards available for the protection of these rights through publications, the media, seminars and other available means.
- To encourage the efforts of non-governmental organisations and institutions working in the field of human rights. It may also undertake such other functions as it may consider necessary for the promotion of Human Rights.

Education for Human Rights

Education has been specified as one of the fundamental Human Rights in Article 26 of the Universal Declaration of Human Rights.

Article 26: (i) Everyone has the right to education. Education shall be free, at least in the elementary and fundamental stages. Technical and professional education shall be equally accessible to all on the basis of merit.

(ii) Education shall be directed to the full development of the human personality and to the strengthening of respect for Human Rights and fundamental freedoms.

It shall promote understanding, tolerance and friendship among all nations, racial or religious groups, and shall further the activities of the United Nations for the maintenance of peace.

(iii) Parents have a right to choose the kind of education that shall be given to their children.

Thus, being a Human Right, education has essentially 'to contribute to the development of good Human Rights culture'. This is why all Human Rights documents have stressed the need for education in Human Rights at all important stages, namely policy formulation, curriculum development and actual teaching-learning activities.

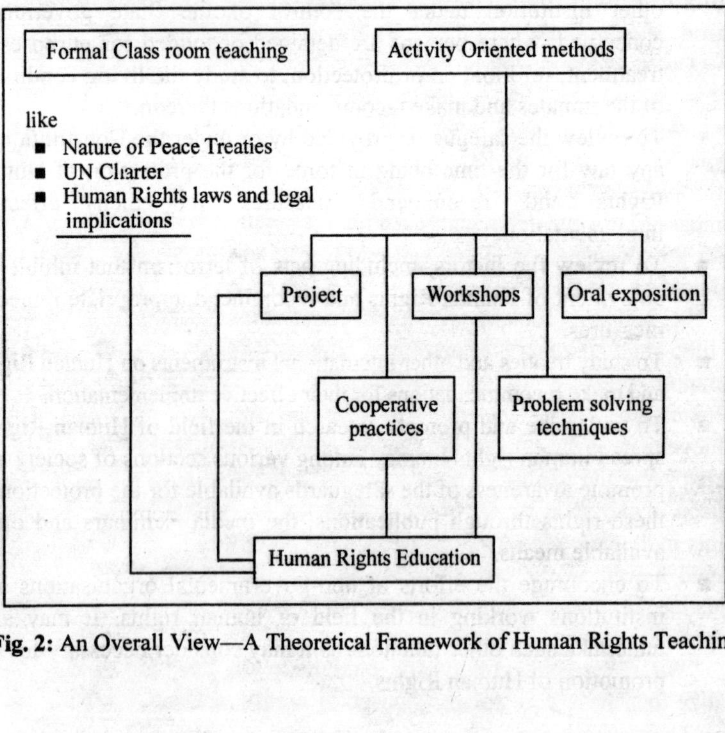

Fig. 2: An Overall View—A Theoretical Framework of Human Rights Teaching

Role of the Teacher in Promoting Human Rights

Every teacher can play an important role in the promotion of the values of Human Rights. The first condition is that he himself not only believes in the Human Rights but also practise in his daily life. In fact the entire work of a teacher relates to the promotion of human rights. He must give due consideration to the personality of the learners. He is expected to teat them justly. He should show no favour to any students. He should cultivate good human relations with his colleges and parents and all others with whom he comes into contact. He should show due interest in all the school programmes, especially related to the promotion of Human Rights. He must keep in mind that duties rightly performed is very conducive to the promotion of Human Rights.

Human Rights or the Rights of the Poor?

"The respect for the dignity of others and desisting from inflicting suffering on them (by way of concentration of power, exploitation and injustice) flow from another kind of anthropology. The human spells differently in the world of victims. In this anthropology, human beings are not primarily ethical beings who follow certain principles of conduct because these are in conformity to reason. There is something even deeper than ethics and reason. *Human beings are those who have deep in them the capacity to be affected by the suffering of others.* It is by awakening this inherent power that we lay a lasting foundation for respect for others and for the removal of their suffering. In other words, human beings are defined not simply in terms of reason; human beings are *compassionate beings.* In this anthropological perspective, human rights are expressions of the compassion for the suffering of the poor. Human suffering and compassion offer the anthropological and spiritual key to interpret human rights as the rights of the poor....

"... humanity remains with many unanswered questions in every sphere of life. The Universal Declaration of Human Rights was supposed to be "a common standard of achievement for all peoples and all nations" ('Preamable', UN Declaration). Whether we can have a sense of achievement at the turn of the century is a disturbing question. Are we not perhaps moving towards a countdown? The crisis of human rights has been caused in the main by the states, which are becoming violators of human rights in alliance with transnational capital and market. Together, they have waged a war on the defenceless poor. Countering these new avatars of injustice is a crucial and critical task before us as committed and responsible citizens in our societies.

"We realize the gravity and complexity of the new task when we realize that these very forces opposed to dignity and human rights are the ones trying to appropriate the human rights and the discourse on them. There is an inherent incompatibility between the market — the symbol of the dominant economy — and the practice of human rights. That is why it is important that human rights become truly the rights in favour of the victims; that they are interpreted with *'positional objectivity'*....

"The restoration of human rights back to the poor calls for certain measures. From a theoretical perspective, debates on the universality of human rights and cultural particularities still retain their validity. But more important today is that such a discourse be related to the concrete social, cultural and political processes. Moreover, the human rights instrumentality needs to be imbued by a spiritual vision that focuses on the *suffering of the victims.* Ultimately we are confronted with the pain inflicted on the poor and the many negations to which they are subjected.

"The more human rights are able to concretely protect the excluded and the poor, the more they will grow in *universality.* Similarly it is through the many struggles of the civil society and social movements that the present set of human rights will become progressively *more comprehensive.* For there are still far too many areas of discrimination against the victims and of violation against their dignity. The effectiveness of the human rights is still in evolution and will depend upon the way each particular society relates them to its own indigenous history of resistance to inhumanity of every kind. Whatever measures are taken, the crucial question remains whether we place the *'sovereignty of the victims'* over that of the state and of the 'free market'. The key to free the human rights from inversions will depend upon this. There are miles to go." *Dr Felix Wilfred*

8.3 CONSTITUTION AND VALUE EDUCATION

Values Enshrined in the Constitution of India

Broadly speaking, the values cherished by the Indian people today are enshrined in the Constitution of India. These permeate the Constitution as a whole. However, following are the most important parts of the Constitution in this regard.

One. The Preamble of the Constitution

Two. Part III dealing with Fundamental Rights

Three. Part IV containing Directive Principles of State Policy.

Four. Part IVA Fundamental Duties

Preamble: This includes:

(i) Secular Values

(ii) Socialist Values

(iii) Democratic Values

These are further detailed:

(a) Justice for all, social, economic and political.

(b) Liberty of thought, belief, expression, belief, faith and worship.

(c) Fraternity.

(d) Regard for the dignity of the individual.

Fundamental Rights: These include:

Equality among individuals.

Directive Principles of State Policy:

(i) Equality between men and women

(ii) Just and humane conditions of work.

Fundamental Duties:

Article 51A. It shall be the duty of every citizen of India:

(a) To promote harmony and the spirit of common brotherhood.

(b) To develop the scientific temper, humanism and the spirit of inquiry and reform.

Recommendations of Committees and Commissions appointed by the Government on the Promotion of Values also

1. Religious Education Committee (1946)
2. University Education Commission (1948-49)
3. Secondary Education Commission (1952-56)
4. Committee on Religious and Moral Education (1959)
5. Education Commission (1964-66)
6. Chavan Committee (1999)

Besides National Policy on Education 1986 and 1992 also made recommendations on the promotion of values.

Definition and Meaning of Moral and Spiritual Values

The Committee on Religious and Moral Education (1959) defined moral and spiritual values as follows:

Moral Value: Anything that helps us to behave properly towards others is of "moral value" (Page 30).

Spiritual Value: Anything that takes us out of ourselves and inspires us to sacrifice for the good of others or for a great cause is of "spiritual value".

National Policy on Education (1986) laid stress on the urgent need for value education in view of the growing erosion of essential values and increasing cynison in society. According to the NPE, education can be a forceful tool for the cultivation of ethical, moral, spiritual and social values. Education should foster universal and eternal values. Value education should help to eliminate obscurantism, religious fanatism, violence superstition and fatalism.

The NPE mentioned the following values: compassion, courage, honesty, tolerance and truthfulness, etc.

Parliamentary Standing Committee popularly known as Chavan Committee [S.B. Chavan was the Chairman of the Committee (1999)]

It listed the following values:

(i) Truth ('*Satya*')
(ii) Religious Conduct ('*Dharma*')
(iii) Peace ('*Shanti*')
(iv) Love ('*Prema*')
(v) Non-violence ('*Ahimsa*')

Integrating Values with Co-curricular Programme

Value education programme should form an integral element of co-curricular programme of the school. In this context, the following programme should receive due attention.

	Instructional Material		*Methods*
1.	Group devotional songs—with simple musical instruments	1.	Guiding group singing
2.	Patriotic songs and folk songs	2.	Choral singing
3.	Sarva Dharma prayers	3.	(a) Group/community singing (b) Silent seating/meditation
4.	Sayings and quotations	4.	Collection, display, reading, recitation, memorisation, group discussion
5.	Short plays and dialogues	5.	Reading, recitation, dramatisation, role-play followed by discussion
6.	Themes for mime	6.	Miming followed by discussion
7.	Incidents, events, episodes from life situations for role-play	7.	Role-play and discussion
8.	Poems and passages for recitation	8.	Collection, display, recitation, reading, writing memorisation, discussion, assignment in forms of question-answer
9.	Passages and episodes from biographies and auto-biographies	9.	Collection, reading, writing, discussion and summarisation
10.	Stories-fables, parables, myths, folk tales, fairy tales, animal tales, etc.	10.	Collection, reading, dramatisation, picturisation and making kits like masks, costumes, etc.
11.	Descriptions of places—cultural, historical, religious, scientific, industrial and of national importance including zoos, museums, etc.	11.	Collection of materials and pictures, reading of materials, discussion, observations and recording and writing reports

(*Contd.*)

Instructional Material	*Methods*
12. Selection from literature—novels, essays, etc.	12. Selection, reading, writing, summarising, passages, picking up significant statements and incidents etc.
13. Descriptions of life styles of various lands and faiths	13. Collection, reading, discussion, presenting the significant details, interviewing, experiencing living in families with people of different life styles
14. Periodicals for pupils and teacher	14. Selection of appropriate material from periodicals for discussion and presentation, paper clipping, scrap books, etc.
15. (a) Slides, (b) film strips, (c) films, (d) tapes, (e) records	15. Preparation, demonstration and feed-back discussion
16. Charts, pictures, posters and models	16. Preparation, display, use and discussion
17. Material such as write-ups, pictures, models of festivals (a) national, (b) religious	17. Selection, reading, discussion, assignment, participation and celebrations (including exhibitions)
18. Quiz and games to give learning experience	18. Organising and conducting
19. Equipment and material for activities such as (i) cultural, (ii) recreational, (iii) social service, (iv) creative, etc.	19. Preparation and use
20. First-aid kit	20. Learning, participating and using appropriately
21. Museums	21. Collections, development and use

8.4 CONSTITUTION AND EDUCATION OF WOMEN

Constitutional Provisions

The following Articles relate to the promotion of values:

Part III—Fundamental Rights

Article 15: Prohibition of discrimination on grounds of religion, race, caste, sex or place of birth.

1. The State shall not discriminate against any citizen on grounds only of religion, race, caste, sex, place of birth or any of them.

2. No citizen shall, on grounds only of religion, race, caste, sex, place of birth or any of them, be subject to any disability, liability, restriction or condition with regard to—

(a) Access to shops, public restaurants, hotels and places of public entertainment; or

(b) The use of wells, tanks, bathing ghats, roads and places of public resort maintained wholly or partly out of State funds or dedicated to the use of the general public.

3. Nothing in this article shall prevent the State from making any special provision for women and children.

Article 16: Equality of opportunity in matters of public employment

(2) No citizen shall, on grounds only of religion, race, caste, sex, descent, place of birth, residence or any of them, be ineligible for, or discriminated against in respect of, any employment or office under the State.

Right against Exploitation

Article 23: Prohibition of traffic in human beings and forced labour

(1) Traffic in human beings and beggar and other similar forms of forced labour are prohibited and any contravention of this provision shall be an offence punishable in accordance with law.

Part IV—Directive Principles of State Policy

Article 39: Certain principles of policy to be followed by the State

The State shall, in particular, direct its policy towards securing:

(a) That the citizens, men and women equally have the right to an adequate means of livelihood;

(b) That there is equal pay for equal work for both men and women;

(c) That health and strength of workers, men and women, and the tender age children are not abused and that citizens are not forced by economic necessity to enter avocations unsuited to their age or strength.

Article 42: *Provision for just and humane conditions of work and maternity relief*

The state shall make provision for securing just and humane conditions for work and maternity relief.

Article 44: *Uniform civil code for citizens*

The State shall endeavour to secure for all citizens a uniform civil code throughout the territory of India.

Part XV—Elections

Article 325: No person to be ineligible for inclusion in, or to claim to be included in a special, electoral roll on grounds of religion, race, caste or sex.

There shall be one general electoral roll for every territorial constituency for election to either House of Parliament or to the either House of the Legislature of a State and no person shall be ineligible for inclusion in any such roll or claim to be included in any special electoral roll for any such constituency on grounds only of religion, race, caste, sex or any of them.

Milestones Towards Women Education and Empowerment in Independent India

I. *Major Committees and Commissions having Bearing on Education*

Following Committees and Commissions have discussed the various issues relating to women's education:

1. The University Education Commission (1948-49).
2. Smt. Durgabai Deshmukh Committee (1959).
3. Smt. Hansa Mehta Committee (1962).
4. M. Bhaktvatsalam Committee to look into the causes of Public Support particularly in Rural Areas for girls Education and to enlist Public Cooperation.
5. Education Commission (1964-66).
6. Resolution on the National Policy on Education (1968).
7. Report of the Committee on the status of Women in India (1974).
8. Challenge of Education 1985.
9. National Policy on Education 1986 (Modified Policy 1992).
10. Programme of Action 1986 and 1992.

NPE (1986 and 1992) and Programme of Action (1992)

Education will be used as an agent of basic charge in the status of women. In order to neutralise the accumulated distortions of the past, there will be a conceived edge in favour of women. The National Education System will play a positive, interventionist role in the development of women. It will foster the development of new values through redesigned curricula, textbooks, the training and orientation of teachers, decision makers and administrators, and the active involvement of educational institutions. This will be an act of faith and social engineering. Women's studies will be promoted as a part of various courses and educational institutions encouraged to take up active programmes to further Women's development.

II. Acts Passed in Independent India

S. No.	*Year*	*Act/Effort*	*Details*
1.	1951	Farm Labour Act	Providing break to working women for nursing children
2.	1952	Employee's State Regulations Act	Providing maternity facilities to women
3.	1956	Beedi and Cigarette Employees Act	Providing child care system at the place of work.
4.	1961	Prematernity Care Act	Providing for abortion and maternity leave

5.	1976	Contract Labour Act	Regulating working hours and maximum 9 hour's work
6.	1976	Equal Wages Act	Providing for equal wages for man and woman
7.	1976	Child Marriage Prohibition Act	Providing for abolition of child marriage
8.	1979	Inter State Migrant Workers Act	Providing for separate public toilet facilities for women
9.	1986	Women Vulgarity Prohibition Act	Providing for prevention of vulgar exhibition of woman-hood
10.	1961	Dowry Prohibition Act (Amend-ment Act 1986)	Prohibition of dowry, providing for strengthening enforcement
11.	1987	Sati Prohibition Act, 1987	Providing for banning Sati prac-tice
12.	1993	73rd and 74th Constitutional Amendment Act	Providing for 30 per cent reser-vation for women in Panchayats
13.	1994	Pre-Natal Diagnostic Technique (Regulation and Prevention of Misuse Act)	Providing for prevention of determination of female foetus in the womb of the mother as illegal
14.	2006	Protection of Women from Domestic Violence Act	Providing safeguards for women

Education for Women's Equality and Empowerment

The NPE 1986 stipulates that "Education will be used as an agent of basic change in the status of women. In order to neutralise the accumulated distortion of the past, there will be a well-conceived edge in favour of women". For achieving this, "The National Education System will play a positive, interventionist role in the empowerment of women". The NPE's programme includes the following dimensions:

1. Redesigning of courses to develop new values.
2. Redesigning of textbooks to eliminate all sex bias.
3. Training and orientation of teachers for developing sensitiveness to women's issues and their empowerment.
4. Orientation of decision-makers and administrators to women issues.
5. Active involvement of educational institutions in enabling women in the process of empowerment of women.
6. According priority to the removal of illiteracy among women through provision of special support services, setting of time-bound targets and effective monitoring.
7. Increasing participation of women in vocational, technical and progressional education at all levels.
8. Following policy of non-discrimination to eliminate stereotyping in vocational and professional courses.

9. Promoting women's participation in non-traditional as well as in existing and emergent technologies.

Mahila Samakhya (MS) *Programme*

The Programme launched in support of Women's education as envisaged in NPE revolves around the Sangha (Village Level Women's Collective) which is considered as the nodal point. The process of mobilising women and creating an environment for women participation in learning is facilitated by a Sahayogni (a cluster coordinator in-charge of 10 villages). She is a crucial link between the village Sangha and the district implementation unit of the programme. The district implementation unit provides resource support and inputs to meet the needs of women. The district units in turn are supported by a state office.

Mahila Samakhya has expanded its coverage to 40 districts and over 7,000 villages.

The Sangha, the nodal point of the programme, addresses a wide range of issues relating to the livelihood of women, their education, health, etc. It has taken an active lead in enrolling children, primarily girls, in the village schools.

Achievements Since 1950-51

Table 1: Percentage of Girls Enrolment to Total Enrolment by Stages

Year	*Primary (Classes I-V)*	*Upper Primary (Classes VI to VIII)*	*Secondary/Sr. Secondary/Intermediate (Classes IX-XII)*	*Higher Secondary (Degree or Above)*
1950-1951	28.1	16.1	13.3	10.0
2004-2005	46.7	44.4	41.5	39.4

Table 2: Gross Enrolment Ratio (GER) Since 1950-51

	1950-51			2004-05		
	Boys	*Girls*	*Total*	*Boys*	*Girls*	*Total*
I. Primary (I-V)	60.6	24.8	42.6	110.7	104.7	107.8
II. Upper Primary (VI to VIII)	20.6	4.6	12.7	74.3	65.1	69.9
III. Elementary (I-VIII)	46.4	17.7	32.1	96.9	89.9	93.5

Table 3: Drop-out Rates Since 1960-61

	1960-61			2004-05		
	Boys	*Girls*	*Total*	*Boys*	*Girls*	*Total*
I. Primary (I-V)	61.7	70.9	64.9	31.8	15.42	29.00
II. Elementary (I to VIII)	75.0	85.0	78.3	50.49	51.28	50.84
III. Secondary (I-IX)	NA	NA	NA	60.41	63.88	61.92

Observations

- The gap in male-female ratio has decreased from 24.84 per cent in 1991 to 21.60 per cent in 2001.
- Female literacy increased by 14.41 per cent i.e. from 39.29 per cent to 53.7 per cent whereas male literacy increased by 11.17 per cent i.e. from 64.13 per cent to 75.30 per cent during the last decade.
- Gender equity and women's empowerment is also visible as about 60 per cent of participants and beneficiaries are women.

Department of Women and Child Development

A separate Department for Women and Child Development was set up at the Centre in 1985 to give a distinct identity and provide a nodal point on matters relating to women's development.

National Institute of Public Cooperation and Child Development

The National Institute of Public Cooperation and Child Development (NIPCCD) is an autonomous organisation functioning under the aegis of the Department of Women and Child Development as its technical arm. The objectives of NIPCCD are to develop and promote voluntary action in social development, conduct a comprehensive review of child development and development and promote programmes in pursuance of the National Policy for Children. It also seeks to develop measures for coordination of government and voluntary action in social development and evolve a common framework for organising children's programmes by government and voluntary welfare action.

Central Social Welfare Board

The Central Social Welfare Board (CSWB) was set up in 1953 with the objective of promoting social welfare activities and implementing welfare programmes for women, children and the handicapped through voluntary organisations. The CSWB is unique in the sense that it was the first organisation in post-Independence era to achieve people's participation for implementation of welfare programmes for women and children through non-governmental organisations (NGOs). Presently more than 18,000 NGOs are receiving financial assistance and guidance from the Board. The programmes implemented by the Board include: socio-economic programme for needy/destitute women, condensed courses of education and vocational training courses for women and girls, awareness generation projects for rural and poor women, family counselling centres/voluntary action bureaux, holiday camps for children, welfare extension projects in border areas, and balwadis, crèches and hostels for working women, etc.

Index